CASE STUDIES IN

CULTURAL ANTHROPOLOGY

GENERAL EDITORS

George and Louise Spindler

STANFORD UNIVERSITY

The Magars of Banyan Hill

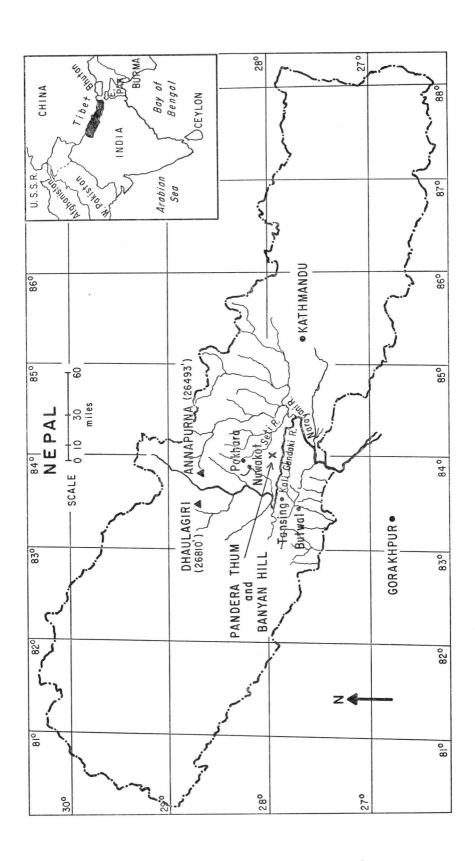

THE MAGARS OF
BANYAN HILL

By

JOHN T. HITCHCOCK
University of California, Los Angeles

HOLT, RINEHART AND WINSTON

NEW YORK   CHICAGO   SAN FRANCISCO   TORONTO   LONDON

TO EMILY AND MARION

Illustration on cover is of the Hill Village headman.

Foreword

About the Series

These case studies in cultural anthropology are designed to bring to students in the social sciences insights into the richness and complexity of human life as it is lived in different ways and in different places. They are written by men and women who have lived in the societies they write about and who are professionally trained as observers and interpreters of human behavior. The authors are also teachers, and in writing their books they have kept the students who will read them foremost in their minds. It is our belief that when an understanding of ways of life very different from one's own is gained, abstractions and generalizations about social structure, cultural values, subsistence techniques, and the other universal categories of human social behavior become meaningful.

About the Author

John Hitchcock, who holds a Ph.D. from Cornell, is an Associate Professor of Anthropology at University of California, Los Angeles and Co-Director, Himalayan Border Countries Project, Institute of International Relations, University of California. He has done fieldwork in Utah on the Uintah-Ouray Reservation, in north India (1953–1955), and in Nepal (1960–1962). Beside articles based on his research in India and Nepal, his publications include *The Rajputs of Khalapur,* written with Leigh Triandis, and a guide for fieldworkers in India, written with Alan Beals. He and his wife Patricia have produced a series of films based on aspects of village life in north India and Nepal and designed as teaching aids for anthropologists.

About the Book

This is a case study of a people who have occupied and used their land for centuries, who have changed the very shape of the mountain upon which they live with their terraces, who have worn footpaths connecting farmsteads deep into the soil, and whose stone resting platforms for wayfarers are enclosed by the great roots of the banyan trees planted long ago to provide shade. They are a people who have no legends of origin from another place. They feel they belong where they are, and indeed they do, for the people fit the land and the land fits them. And not only do the people live on their land as they feel they always have, but their many godlings that control life and the resources upon which life is based are at home there also and must be treated with regular sacrifices of food.

We begin the reading of this book with this sense of belonging and permanence. As we read on and our understanding grows, we find that the people of Banyan Hill are also dependent upon each other; the forms of this interdependence are made clear as the individuals and groups are described.

The author has achieved a remarkable resolution of the potential conflict in every description of a way of life between "sensuous reality," as he phrases it, and the abstractions with which we try to order that reality. We are given the details that make it possible to understand behavior. It is as though we, the readers, were there on Banyan Hill. The intimacy of our contact with reality is compelling and intriguing. And yet we do not get lost in a labyrinth of meaningless detail at any point in our journey. There is order in the facts as presented. There is a way of life, not merely fragmented bits of behavior. But the ordering is never obtrusive. The abstractions are in the author's mind, and he skillfully uses them in his ordering of observations; in doing so, he never blunts the senses of the reader by reifying the abstractions, as though they, the abstractions, were indeed reality.

GEORGE AND LOUISE SPINDLER
General Editors

Stanford, California
November 1965

Acknowledgment

Fieldwork in Nepal was supported by the National Science Foundation, and I owe the Foundation a special debt of gratitude for making possible a six-month extension of my stay. For permission to do the research and for many courtesies I am deeply grateful to the Government of His Majesty, the King of Nepal. The list of people to whom I am indebted for assistance in my work and their many kindnesses to me and my family is too long for inclusion here. Rather than make omissions I prefer to make full acknowledgment in a subsequent work. It would be impossible, however, not to mention High School Master Hem Bahadur Thapa, who assisted me so ably throughout the research among his people; or my wife, a constant companion and helper, who among a mountain people noted for hardihood, courage, good humor, and respect for man's common humanity, was recognized always, although a stranger, as somehow one of their very own.

Contents

Contents

A major portion of Pandera Thum, looking north.

One of the hamlets in Pandera Thum. The view is to the south.

The headman of Banyan Hill (in white to right) holds a council of arbitration on a trailside resting place.

Above: Dambar Singh, lama, in a state of possession in Maila Ba's courtyard. The contents of his medicine kit are beside him.

Left: Nachari dancers are celebrating the life of Lord Krishna in the Adamara headman's courtyard.

During the naming ceremony, Dev Bahadur watches while his *pandit* blows a name into his daughter's ear. The eleven-day-old baby is being held by her sister. The little boy is her brother.

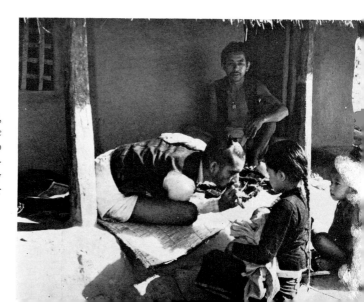

Introduction

THIS book is a preliminary report on a portion of my research in Nepal. In 1954 and again in 1955 while trekking in the Himalayas, I had noted a marked difference in tone and tenor of life between communities at high altitudes and those at low. It was easy to believe that the difference in height and associated physical environment had something to do with what I saw and felt. This early experience in the mountains posed a question, and a major reason for going to Nepal in 1960-62 was to see whether it was possible to determine with any precision how communities were affected by differences in their physical environment.

I assumed there were factors besides geographical location that caused communities to differ from one another, and if possible I wanted to hold them constant. They consisted of: (1) the cultural genesis of the peoples living in the communities; (2) innovations made in one community and not shared with others; and (3) outside cultural features either imposed by the political setting during the course of history or offered by diffusion, including contact with peoples who had a different origin.

In an attempt to control these factors, I went to Nepal where I knew a number of Tibeto-Burman-speaking tribes had penetrated from the north, covering areas on the southern Himalayan slopes where there was much variation in topography. For a variety of reasons, the Magars turned out to be the tribe best suited at that time for the project I had in mind.

On the basis of a month's preliminary trek into Magar country northwest of Pokhara, I decided that contrasting environments led to two quite different types of Magar communities. There were those whose members moved from a lower winter village to high summer pastures where they grazed their livestock and planted potatoes. One reason for the move, which involved many males and a few females during most of the spring and summer, was that fodder from sources near the lower village only lasted from fall until spring. In this type of community, even the winter villages were above 6000 feet, making it impossible

1

to grow good crops of millet or irrigated rice. The other type of community was completely sedentary. Throughout the year, there were sources near the village that provided ample fodder for livestock. In addition, altitude, terrain, and water permitted good crops of both millet and irrigated rice.

I selected Banyan Hill as an example of the latter type of Magar community, and during two months of trekking at different times in 1961–1962, I located an example of the second type about ten days walk to the northwest. Saying this is tantamount to a denial that Banyan Hill can be regarded as a representative Magar community. To a degree this is true and in a subsequent publication I hope to examine in some detail the differences between it and the more northerly village. But Banyan Hill is enough like any other Magar community I visited or learned about south of the main Himalayan ridge to enable one, using knowledge derived from it, clearly to distinguish Magar communities north or south, high or low, from neighboring communities inhabited by different groups, such as Brahmans, Thakuris, Chetris, Thakalis, Newars, Gurungs, and Tamangs; or artisans such as Metalworkers (Kami), Tailors (Damai), and Leatherworkers (Sarki). In this sense it is a representative community.

If my primary reason for doing research in Nepal and among the Magars was to answer a question about the social and cultural effects of different ecological niches, it was also to explore a region barely known to anthropologists and to learn about the home life of a people whom the world knew primarily as extraordinarily good and tough infantrymen. When first entering a village, and repeatedly throughout my stay there, I used to tell the Magars who were offering us hospitality and permitting us to share their way of life that in my country there was much interest in the Nepalese people. The many reasons for this included not only films of the new king's coronation and Everest and Tensing and Hillary, but also the fact that many had heard of the Gurkha soldiers or perhaps had fought side by side with them in Burma, Africa, or Italy. People who wanted to find out more about these soldiers, especially how they lived at home, found there were very few books—and none based on research conducted for any length of time in the mountain communities where the soldiers lived. I told the villagers I was trying to learn enough to write such a book and wanted it to be a true account. They understood this aim, and many Magars in Banyan Hill and elsewhere gave hours of their time to help me achieve it. I hope I have.

In writing this book, I also have tried to convey a sense of the essence of fieldwork—that tension between sensuous reality, especially as expressed in the uniqueness of individuals and events, and those abstractions with which we try to capture it and give it order.

1

Tribesmen and Farmers

The Magar Tribe

A LTHOUGH there is good reason to think that the Magars are one of the most numerous tribes of Nepal, there is no basis for an accurate estimate of their number. There are Magar enclaves scattered throughout the country, but most are concentrated in a single sector. To locate this area, it is useful to think of the topographical features of Nepal as bands of latitude and longitude whose intersections will provide us with general boundaries. Latitudinally, Nepal is divided into four zones. The most southerly is the low, damp, tropical forest area that adjoins India. Moving north one comes to a broad mountainous region, deeply incised by thousands of rivers and streams. The land here slopes upward to the north so that the valley floors increase in altitude from 2000 feet or less to some that are 10,000 feet or more. The hills and mountain ridges vary correspondingly from about three thousand feet to more than fifteen thousand feet. The perpetual snows of the towering Himalayan mountain chain form the next topographical feature, and beyond the snows is the high barren plateau where Nepal merges into Tibet.

Longitudinally, Nepal is divided by a number of great river systems, all tributary to the Indian Ganges. One of these rivers, the Kali Gandaki (and later the Narayani), drains an area that includes the central portion of Nepal. Its waters come mostly from the melting snows and the lower slopes of two immense ranges, the Dhaulagiri and Annapurna Himals. The Magar homeland is the middle mountain belt drained by the Narayani and its tributaries. One cannot travel very far anywhere in this area without encountering Magar shelters in high mountain pastures or Magar villages on mountain slopes and hilltops.

When one takes the long view of Magars who inhabit this region, one notices traits they have in common. They pursue a form of mixed agriculture and combine stock-raising with growing crops in fertilized fields. All observe caste restrictions and claim to be Hindus. All observe a marriage rule that forbids an

3

alliance with the daughter of the father's sister but encourages one with the daughter of the mother's brother. And most Magars, as one of their two languages, speak a tongue that is part of a large Asian language family, Tibeto-Burmese.

However, when one takes a closer view, differences appear, especially on each side of a line that divides their homeland roughly into northern and southern halves. The Magar tribe is split into a number of subtribes. In the southern half of the region, the subtribes that predominate almost to the exclusion of any others are the Ale, Rana, Thapa, and Burathoki; it was in this southern area, anciently called the Bara Mangranth, that Magars first made their appearance in written history. During the twelfth century, they sacked the Kathmandu Valley that long had been the seat of urban, civilized culture in Nepal. Almost all Magars in this area carry on sedentary agriculture with emphasis on millet, maize, and in many areas, irrigated rice. The influence of Hinduism is strong, and as their house language the Magars here speak a Tibeto-Burman dialect called Magarkura.

Magars in the northern half of the area belong to a different group of subtribes. Here one finds the Bura, Gharti, Pun, and Rokha. They also grow maize, and at lower altitudes grow irrigated rice; because most of them live at higher altitudes than Magars further south, there is more emphasis upon crops such as barley and potatoes, which are better suited to cold. There is more stock herding in the north, and some Magars follow a transhumant pattern, living at one place during the winter and shifting with their herds to high pastures during the summer. Northern Magars have been more lightly touched by Hinduism. Not all of them have retained an indigenous home language, but those who have speak a Tibeto-Burman dialect called Kamkura. It resembles Magarkura but the two languages are not mutually intelligible.

Magar origins are lost in obscurity. The tribe seems to have been part of a very ancient influx of Mongoloid, Tibeto-Burman-speaking peoples into Nepal, probably from the north and east. It also seems probable, in view of differences between its northern and southern halves, that the tribe represents two different streams of migration.

The Magar hamlet of Banyan Hill is situated on the southern slope of a mountain close to the center of the Magar homeland; from the 4000 foot ridge that rises above its scattered farmsteads, one can see the massive white wall of Annapurna about thirty-five air miles away to the north. Looking south thirty-five miles, one can see the last of the middle ranges where they blend with the horizon near the Indian border. In the legends of many peoples of the world there are stories that tell how they came from some distant land to their present home. The Magars of Banyan Hill have no such legend. When asked where they came from they answer, "We have lived here always." Although they may preface a remark by saying, "When we came here . . .," they never say where they came *from.* Banyan Hill, or some unspecified nearby place, always has been home to them. They feel they are living in the place where they belong.

BANYAN HILL MAGARS

There were twenty-four farmsteads in Banyan Hill; each with its head or central figure was different from any of the others. The pattern that emerged in the mind as Banyan Hill gradually changed from a collection of people and buildings to a community began with a sense of the uniqueness of each individual farmstead and the family members who lived there.

The first group of families was called Darkang. It was a segment of a larger lineage of Thapas whose most prominent member was the Banyan Hill headman. Darkang was the lowest cluster of houses in Banyan Hill and was graced with an unusually fine spring.

DARKANG

Dev Bahadur   Dev Bahadur was the only adult man in this group of five houses at the southwestern end of Banyan Hill. An ex-soldier, but poor and driven to work as plowman and field laborer for well-to-do Brahman neighbors, he almost always wore the increasingly threadbare army khaki jacket in which he was mustered out. His mother, the oldest person in the village, spent her days in her own nearby house. She would sit huddled by the fire on cold days or on the ground outside when it was sunny and hot, baring her sticklike arms and legs to the sun. Her eldest son had gone to India and never returned, and tales of a dimming past brought her to tears whenever we went to sit with her. Twice a day Dev Bahadur's wife or his young daughter brought the old woman the little food she could eat.

Dubal Singh   Dev Bahadur's brother, Dubal Singh, had gone to India in search of work. He left a wife and children at each end of a house he had scrupulously divided down the center, as he had all of his land and property. His rare letters, written by a professional letter writer, were addressed to both wives, and in them too there was scrupulous division: The elder wife should sacrifice a chicken to Black Bhairam for the health of the son born to her soon after he left; the younger wife should sacrifice a chicken to Barahi so that the family would prosper and he would find work. The elder wife approached that rarity—a fat hill woman. The younger wife distilled for sale the best millet liquor in Banyan Hill.

Sita Devi   Up the slope from these two women there were two others, one a widow and the other waiting for the return of a husband gone to India for work. Sita Devi, childless and the neatest housekeeper and most stylish dresser in Banyan Hill, had been waiting for four years for her husband to come back from Assam. The two letters she had had since he had gone had not said what his work was, but a returned hillman who had seen him had told her he was a railroad guard. She was an excellent manager, and could rely for help on an attentive brother from a village a half-day's walk away. Her husband had sent no money and she had needed none.

When Sita Devi was a young girl her father had married the woman who later became Dubal Singh's younger wife. There was a daughter from this marriage, a plump and winsome girl who had married young and left her husband. Named Ganga, she ate her meals with her mother at Dubal's house, but spent most of the rest of the time at Sita Devi's. She was a close friend of the three unmarried daughters of a Magar headman in the nearby hamlet of Adamara. At night there were frequent gatherings of young people at Sita Devi's house to drink and laugh, flirt and sing until dawn. People said Sita Devi's house always had been a house for singers. Her husband was a noted song leader, a skill he had acquired in compensation perhaps for a deformity of his hand and arm. While playing as a boy, he had fallen from a tree and broken his arm. No one in the hills knew how to set so severe a break. Sita, too, was an excellent singer, and it was their singing that had brought the two together and had led to marriage, even though she was older than he. Although now in her late thirty's, Sita still was attractive. It must have been this attractiveness set off by velvet blouses and a gold necklace, that worried the headman of Banyan Hill and led him to reprimand her for having singing parties while her husband, his lineage brother, was away. A woman of great self-sufficiency, she had listened respectfully and had not changed her way of life at all.

Jag Maya Jag Maya lived close to Sita Devi. Very plain and dressed mostly in old white cotton, she was a widow and belonged to the older generation. Her husband had been the uncle (father's brother) of Sita Devi's husband. As a little girl she had gone to India with her father, who was in the British army, and had married a soldier friend of his when she was twelve. This first husband had died, and it was her second husband who had brought her to Banyan Hill. In the six years since his death she had had to sell some of their land to get enough to eat. She knew her farm would not last long enough to keep her solvent during her last years. She had no real brothers, and cherished a family of ritual brothers in a nearby village. One day she honored me by asking me also to become her ritual brother. On Brother-Worship Day in the fall we sat opposite each other and she carefully painted a red, white, yellow and blue design (tikka) on my forehead, gave me a new cap, and bowing with folded hands to touch my feet, wished me good fortune for the coming year.

KUTUMSA

Kanchha Ba Leaving Darkang and walking up the mountainside, one came to another group of five houses called Kutumsa. The first belonged to the Headman's youngest brother, his wife, and five boys. We called the head "youngest uncle on the father's side" (Kanchha Ba). Following the example of his admired eldest brother, the Headman, Kanchha Ba and his wife had become Vaishnavites and were ardent in pursuit of religious perfection. His wife, a slender woman with flashing black eyes, daily made sandalwood paste and carefully painted her forehead with the U-shaped mark of a Vishnu follower and used the paste to stamp his emblems on her body—the sun on her right shoulder, a seashell on her left shoulder, and the God's footprints above each breast. On important holy days Kanchha Ba and his wife walked to the Kali Gandaki River where there was a temple complex for the worship of Krishna, who was one of the manifestations of Vishnu; and every night they came to the Headman's small temple to sing evensong and receive sanctified food from his evening worship, or puja.

Maila Ba The next house belonged to the Headman's second eldest brother, Maila Ba. My wife and I lived four months in his courtyard, on an opensided raised platform with a thatched roof, called a *dhansar*. We were better acquainted with Maila Ba's family, animal and human, than any other in Banyan Hill. He kept his mare under our platform and we were up with her the night she lay groaning on her side in the courtyard and gave birth to a fine black stallion foal. The growing impertinence of a young goat was part of the day's laughter, and when it came time for the cock to be given as promised sacrifice to the Household Godling, we found the predawn darkness empty without his song and proud flapping from the pig pen roof.

In religious matters Maila Ba was the brother who followed the Headman least closely. There were two important strands in the Headman's religious attitude. One strand allied him with the Brahman way of life and was a way of stating, "Though I am a Magar, I follow the Brahman way of life as closely as my caste status permits." Most Magars kept pigs and chickens and ate their meat. These customs were not acceptable to Brahmans and were among those which most clearly set Magars apart from their Brahman neighbors. The Headman observed the Brahman taboo on these animals and in his mind the pig and chicken had come to stand for what he regarded as the Magar's comparative improvidence, lack of education, and religious carelessness.

The second strand allied him with the Vaishnavites and required that in addition to pork and chicken he give up meat of all kinds. His Vaishnavism also placed a taboo upon live sacrifice, smoking, and drinking. Brahmans were not supposed to smoke or drink and few did. But non-Vaishnavite Brahmans officiated at ceremonies in which goats and sheep were sacrificed, though they themselves did not do the actual killing. They also ate the meat of these animals. By dissociating himself from any live sacrifice and from any meat-eating, the Vaishnative Headman was saying in effect, "In some religious matters, I am even more strict than some of my Brahman neighbors."

Maila Ba, who was a pious man, though in a different style, had refused to give up the old ways and was content to be an ordinary Magar. His hookah bubbled on his porch in the evening, and the Headman's sons and the sons of his other brothers used to repair to his kitchen when they and their friends wanted to feast on a goat or a chicken and some liquor.

As a youth Maila Ba had enlisted in the army, but had yielded to his eldest brother's monthly written requests to come home and help manage the family estate—a task the young Headman found less and less possible to pursue the more heavily he became engaged in local politics. Even at sixty Maila Ba was a good-looking man with thin sensitive features. He had retained the body of an athlete, and though nearly blind, still climbed for leaf fodder to the top of the tallest trees. There was a family of Ex-Slaves living just behind his cattle shed. They had two sons, and both were feeble-minded. The elder, a boy of seventeen was devoted to Maila Ba, and when the boy flew into occasional rages, threw stones at the person he thought had crossed him, and retreated high into a tree, only Maila Ba could calm him and get him to come down. During the heat of the day they napped together on the same straw mat under one of Maila Ba's trees.

Maila Ba was a man of great good humor and had married seven times. Only three wives were on the scene. He lived with two of them and the eleven year old daughter of a third. The latter had gone to a neighboring village to keep house for a son who was a widower. The eldest wife was forty-five, and the newest, a strong, conscientious girl he had married a year before, twenty-four. Maila Ba had no sons, and it was need for labor to run his large farm which accounted for this late marriage to a young girl. For the most part Maila Ba remained at home with his wives and worked hard. But when there was a marriage he dressed up in a green western-style suitcoat made in Singapore, a gift sent him by his only other child, a daughter married to a soldier serving with the British in Malaya. At wedding festivities he joined the youths in their singing, dancing, and drinking, and on occasion would be helped home by two of them the next day, one on each side, steadying him as he walked humming down the path.

Saila Ba. Third uncle (Saila Ba) lived in two large two-storied houses which faced each other across a courtyard. His farm was situated between Maila Ba and the Headman. If Kanchha Ba followed the Headman's way of life in shared religiosity and Maila Ba represented the traditional Magar way, Saila Ba, like his farmstead, stood in between. Out of respect for his eldest brother and a sense of diplomacy he gave up smoking, drinking, and meat-eating. But he did continue to perform pujas requiring live sacrifice, and for use in these he kept a pig and a cock.

Now an army pensioner, he had held the high rank of Subedar, a junior commissioned officer. He always was addressed by this title and his wife was addressed as Subedarni. He had a married son serving with the British in Malaya. Now that he himself was back from the army for good, he was raising a second crop of children, and was especially proud of the three youngest, who were chubby, healthy boys. A reserved and unobtrusive man, he spent much of his time sitting on a pasture slope outside the village grazing his cows and goats.

The Headman The portly, very dignified Headman was the focal figure in the village and in the region as well. A remarkable man who had educated himself and achieved political preeminence in competition with a Brahman who had advantages of education, caste tradition, and political preferment, he now, in the closing years of his life, had turned to religion with all the intensity with which he had earlier pursued wealth and power. His three former wives had died and he was married to a fourth, a sturdy woman in her early forties with a sing-song tune in her speech. He had ten living children and an eleventh was born during our stay. His eldest son, with two young wives, and his third eldest son, newly married, were living with him in the same house, though eating in separate kitchens. The household also included two of his wife's young relatives, who had come from their village to go to school in Banyan Hill.

The Headman always was awake before dawn, and he and his wife went together to bathe at the spring. Every morning and evening, with the help of a white-bearded Brahman retainer who also formed part of his household, he did two lengthy pujas, signalizing their closing phases with blasts on a conch shell, that in power and unvarying pattern were recognized everywhere as unmistakably his. He did most of his account-keeping and writing of legal documents while sitting in a corner of his second-storey porch. People who came to consult him would wait below in the courtyard and his wife would give them corn to husk or grass to twist into rope. He never sat to talk without doing some work with his hands, and he always dressed like a simple hill farmer. Frequently he was called to other villages for consultation, and he made these trips on a sturdy brown pony.

Havildar Major The last house in the main Kutumsa group belonged to the Havildar Major, a pensioner whose rank was equivalent to first sergeant. The Havildar was neither rich nor poor. In the past year or two, since his eldest son had grown up enough to help him with such heavy work as improving his paddy fields, his farm had begun to break even. In this sense the Havildar was the typical farmer of Banyan Hill. He was also a typical Magar in appearance. About five feet tall, he was brown-skinned, short, stocky, and wiry. His round face, with its definite Mongoloid cast, told of an ancestry whose place of origin ultimately was Inner Asia or China. Both he and his wife could cover twenty miles a day barefoot over steep mountain trails. Like all men of the hamlet, he wore a cotton shirt with ties, a cummerbund, and a short canvas skirt. His heavily muscled thighs were eloquent testimony to the strength his way of life required and engendered. In religious matters the Havildar believed in the seemliness of traditional ways. In this respect he was like Maila Ba, and the two of them, occasionally joined by Saila Ba, carefully carried out observances from which the Headman and Kanchha Ba had turned away. He had a strong sense of craftsmanship and made the best wicker baskets in Banyan Hill.

Dirgha Singh Dirgha Singh was the Havildar's father's brother's son. He lived on an isolated farmstead across a gully and up a hillside from the Havildar and the rest of Kutumsa. He had separated himself both spatially and socially from his lineage. There were a number of disagreements which had brought this about, but the basic reason may well have been Dirgha's feeling that he should have been headman. It is said that Dirgha's grandfather lost the headmanship when he displeased his father and left home. The father gave the office to his younger son and from him it descended to the present headman. Whatever the reason, Dirgha moved mostly in an orbit which included his affinal relatives in a nearby community. He looked like the Havildar Major, but he had no teeth and this made him look much older. A humorous man, his eyes flickered back and forth laterally while he talked.

CHEPTE

The Thapas of Kutumsa and Darkang said they brought a group of Rana Magars with them when they first came to Banyan Hill. These Ranas lived in a section of Banyan Hill called Chepte and were traditional in-laws of the Thapas. "We said to them," claimed the Thapas, "since you like to hunt, go and live near us on that eastern ridge where there is heavy forest, and we will send you our daughters."

A lack of men in Darkang made it difficult for the people there to carry out some of the functions normally associated with a lineage segment, and the differences in religious views between the Headman and his second brother and the Havildar Major weakened such ties and activities in Kutumsa. Neither condition was present in Chepte so that lineage ties were strong, and the people's solidarity was further enhanced by shared poverty. Almost as if to signalize their cohesiveness, the families of Chepte built many of their houses close together.

Shri Ram Shri Ram was the oldest man and the leader of the Rana group. Though extremely thin and too feeble to do much fieldwork, he still actively played the role of elder in Chepte and was the key to its cohesion. He lived with his young daughter-in-law and her baby. The girl had been married to a soldier but fell in love with Shri Ram's second son, Narpati, while her husband was away in the army. When the husband returned and found his wife pregnant, he turned her out and threatened to kill Narpati if he caught him. The frightened son had run away to India. Shri Ram's only daughter had become the second wife of the Headman's eldest son.

Ek Bahadur Ek Bahadur was Shri Ram's elder son. He was about thirty-five and his house formed part of a cluster that included all the Ranas belonging to Shri Ram's lineage. He had twin boys, the only living twins in Banyan Hill. Seeing Ek Bahadur and his children, all of whom were thin, reminded one that his father's extreme thinness, though somewhat exaggerated by age, must have been an inherited trait. Ek Bahadur had a finger ring with a bit of gold inlay in the crown. It could be used for making "gold water," which was useful for removing ritual pollution. He always wore it fastened to one of the ties on his shirt.

Dhem Bahadur Dhem Bahadur was the orphaned son of Shri Ram's younger brother. He was in his late teens and worked his own farm and Shri Ram's as well. Despite this responsibility, he was a gay blade. At night he attended all the young people's dances and sings, and during the day he was often out blasting away at pigeons with his shotgun. His carefree ways drove one wife away, but he quickly got another, despite the mother's very strong opposition. He was the son of the sister of the Banyan Hill headman and found it easy to secure the Headman's help. When his wife ran away, the Headman helped him secure compensation from her new husband and also worked to lessen the opposition of the new wife's mother.

Lakshmi Devi A house not far from Shri Ram's belonged to the widow,

Lakshmi Devi. Her husband, who was the son of Shri Ram's father's second brother, had died three years before, leaving her with six children. The eldest son, who was nineteen, was the main breadwinner. He worked as plowman for a Brahman; the next youngest son, who was thirteen, helped the same Brahman by doing other kinds of fieldwork, occasionally being joined by his mother. Despite all their work, they were a very poor family, and more often than any other family in the hamlet, their meals consisted of boiled maize rather than rice.

Bal Bahadur　Shri Ram's father's third brother had a son named Bal Bahadur, and he lived on the other side of Shri Ram, near Dhem Bahadur. Though younger than Shri Ram, he looked almost as old and wizened. He had a pretty daughter of fifteen, and her outgoing beaming vitality made Bal and his wife, both of whom were very quiet and withdrawn, seem even more so.

There was another segment of Shri Ram's patrilineage in Chepte. No one knew exactly how the two segments were related, except that the tie came down from an ancestor shared long ago and forgotten. This second segment consisted of two brothers, Teg Bahadur and Padam Bahadur.

Teg Bahadur　Teg Bahadur was an ex-soldier who served in Burma during the last war. Since he did not serve out his full term of enlistment, he had no pension. Like his brother, he was very tall for a Magar (about 5'9") and was married to a girl he towered over. Teg and his wife had no children. With his wife's permission he tried twice to bring a second wife into the house. But when the new wives actually had taken up residence, the first wife was so jealous and made life so miserable for them and Teg too, that both quickly left. Teg and his wife spent much time at the home of the brother and were very close to his children. They also looked after Teg's wife's mother, Dil Maya.

Dil Maya　When Dil Maya's husband died, her only son, who was twenty-six and a soldier, came home from the army and then also died. Lonely and in need of help in her own village, which was about a half hour's walk from Chepte, she gave her son-in-law a loan and in return he provided her with land, a buffalo shed, and a house. He farmed for her and gave her a share of the produce, including leaves or grass for her buffalo every day. Like the headman of Banyan Hill, Dil Maya had become a Vaishnavite. In her courtyard she kept a tulsi plant, which is sacred to Vishnu, and morning and evening did puja before it. Her best friend was a young widow from the nearby Metalworker hamlet. She and this woman used to sit together on Dil Maya's porch in the evening, gossiping and occasionally singing together songs that were popular among youths two or three decades ago.

Padam Bahadur　Padam Bahadur, Teg's elder brother, was a heavy set, slow-moving man with moustaches hanging down each side of his mouth. He spoke with extreme deliberateness in a high-pitched husky voice. After Padam's first wife had died and left him with a number of children, one of his relatives persuaded a woman from a distant village to leave her husband and come to his house as a wife. She was jolly and loud, with a sharp tongue, and she sometimes referred to Padam, in his presence, as "Bainsi Bahadur," which meant literally, brave buffalo. She asked my wife to become her ritual sister, and once the ceremony of exchange of rupees was complete, we had a circle of kinsmen that included all of Chepte.

Bom Bahadur   The other houses of Banyan Hill were not strictly part of either the Thapa or the Rana lineages. Bom Bahadur, who lived below the Rana houses, participated in most of their activities and was regarded as a distant affinal relative by the Rana men. He had come to Banyan Hill when his wife's father died without male issue, and his household included his mother-in-law. It also included the wife of his eldest son, who was serving in the Indian army, and his second son and wife. Bom Bahadur was an ex-soldier and had worked as a hill recruiter for the British.

There were two sisters of the Headman who lived in Banyan Hill, one near the Ranas and the other near the Thapas of Kutumsa. The Headman's eldest sister, now a childless widow, had moved to Banyan Hill when her husband was still alive. Her husband had purchased some land and the Headman also had given him some. Following his death, she lived alone on her farm and participated as fully as possible in her brother's religious regimen, including attendance mornings and evenings at his two daily pujas. She always wore a wool pullover cap, even on the hottest days, because wool was ritually pure and did not have to be washed before meals. During our stay, she turned over her worldly possessions to the Vaishnavite Brahman who had influenced her brother, and went to live in his ashram, sharing a small riverside hut with another widow.

Tara Maya   The Headman's youngest sister, Tara Maya, had come to Banyan Hill recently, when her husband had abandoned her. Her brother helped provide a farm and a house. She worked the farm with the help of her son, a boy who had begun to think seriously of following his brother into the army. In her youth, this sister had been a good singer and was widely known for her witty rejoinders in songs of repartee. Once she was said to have beaten a boy in a repartee singing contest that lasted three days and nights. Had she lost, the forfeit would have been her hand in marriage.

Indra Kumari   Indra Kumari was another childless widow. After her husband's death, as an act of piety, she gave land to her husband's father's sister's son, Bir Bahadur, another Banyan Hill Magar. She managed the remainder of her farm with the help of an Ex-Slave and his Magar wife, who occupied a shed next to her house. Indra Kumari, another Banyan Hill resident who had become a Vaishnavite, was a close friend of the Headman's eldest sister. She and the wife of the Ex-Slave, who also had been converted, used to join regularly in the sister's religious activities, such as daily attendance at the Headman's pujas. The three women also made frequent trips together to the Kali Gandaki, for ritual bathing. The Ex-Slave, who had run away and served a full term in the British army as a Thapa Magar, resisted his wife's attempts to make him turn Vaishnavite and give up liquor, meat, and tobacco. She only succeeded by denying him her bed.

Santa Prasad   The farm highest on the hill slope belonged to Havildar Santa Prasad, an ex-soldier with twenty years of service, who had fought in

North Africa, where he had been captured by the Germans and later had escaped. He had lost two wives and had only recently married again. He had one child, a baby girl. His father had made the move to Banyan Hill from another nearby village. Since most of his relatives still lived in this village he participated more in their festival activities than in those of Banyan Hill. He was a very hard-working, self-contained man, and was gradually creating an excellent farm.

Bir Bahadur   Bir Bahadur, already mentioned as recipient of a gift of land from Indra Kumari, his maternal uncle's son's wife, was a pensioner, but at the lowest rank. To maintain himself and his family, he worked as plowman for a Brahman. He had fallen from a tree as a boy and his forehead was flattened and badly scarred on one side. Like Dirgha Singh and Santa Prasad, his strongest social ties were with relatives in nearby villages.

Om Bahadur   The final Magar house in Banyan Hill belonged to Om Bahadur. Originally from another village where he had lost all his land, he had come to work for the Headman as plowman and farm hand. In return for his work, the Headman gave him food, cattle, and some land on which to grow his own crops. Om Bahadur, who had married five times, now was living happily with his sixth wife. He was an extremely hard worker, and with the Headman's strong bullocks plowed more land in a day than anyone else in the region. Despite the opposition of her mother, Om Bahadur's step-daughter had run away and married light-hearted Dhem Bahadur in Chepte.

2

Settings

The Settlement Pattern

BANYAN HILL is surrounded by a group of seventeen hamlets that form part of an administrative subdivision called Pandera Thum. In the thum as a whole there are about six hundred households, and if one estimates five persons per household, the population numbers about three thousand. Among the caste groups of which the thum is composed, the Brahmans are the most numerous. Their community consists of 243 households, or approximately 40 percent of the total number of houses. The Magars account for about one hundred and ninety households, or approximately 32 percent, so that between them, Magars and Brahmans represent almost three-fourths of the people in Pandera Thum. Other groups such as the Metalworkers (sixty households), Leatherworkers (thirty-six households), Ex-Slaves (thirty-six households), and Tailors (seventeen households) are much less numerous. The remaining caste groups account for a total of only eighteen houses. Of these, the group of most importance are the Newars (seven households), most of whom keep shops in the thum bazaar.

The various hamlets are situated on hilltops or high on the hillsides and are located near springs. In each hamlet one caste tends to predominate. Brahmans are found almost exclusively in eight, while Magars, though not quite as exclusive, are numerically dominant in six. For the most part, farmsteads are scattered so that hamlet boundaries are a matter of local definition and are not obvious to the eye of a stranger. The few fairly dense clusterings belong as a rule to Metalworkers, Leatherworkers, or Tailors. These artisan-farmers do not own as much land as most Magars and Brahmans, and by grouping their houses close together in one spot they are able to secure more benefit from the land they do have. Hence, looking at the thum from a distant vantage point it is the houses of the artisan-farmers that are most conspicuous. The other more scattered homesteads tend to be hidden by the trees that surround them, so that the thum appears to have many fewer homesteads than it actually has.

All hamlets are connected by footpaths. In most places the paths are paralleled by deciduous trees or rattling stands of bamboo, and often the foliage is so thick that even at midday one walks in shade. Many paths are lined by thorn fences or stone walls and have been worn so deep in places by cattle and rains that the base of the fences and walls are above one's head. Where paths come together, especially on the ridges of hills, there are broad stone platforms. At the time these platforms were built, a banyan or pipal tree was planted in the center, or one of each kind of tree was planted at either end. During the course of centuries the trees have grown until today the root systems of many have almost completely enveloped their platforms. The purpose of these structures, which are one of the thum's most characteristic features, is to provide a shady resting place for travelers. At the top of the platform there are ledges on which those using the trails can set their loads. These structures also provide a meeting place for neighborhood councils, a spot where young people meet to sing, or simply a shady retreat from a hillman's own courtyard where he can go to chat a little with passersby while making a basket or doing some other household chore.

Pandera Thum is fortunate in having many springs with a constant heavy flow from their wooden or stone spouts. Even more than the resting platforms, the springs are centers of neighborhood activity and visiting. It is seldom that one does not find someone at a spring either washing clothes, performing a religious ritual, or drawing water in a large copper jug.

Counting all the houses in the immediate vicinity of Banyan Hill, there are a total of fifty-three, with twenty-three belonging to Metalworkers, three to Ex-Slaves, and one to a Leatherworker. Most of the Metalworker houses and the single Leatherworker house form a cluster northeast of Kutumsa that is referred to as Metalworker Village.

The Basis for Subsistence

If the paths around Pandera Thum, and the resting places, suggest that people have lived here for centuries, so does the land, which is the basis for the way of life. All but the highest and steepest hillsides have been terraced. In many places even the tops of lower hills have been scraped flat, and everywhere as a sign of age, the terraces are level and supported by well-built stone walls. There are two types of terrace, irrigated and nonirrigated. The difference is readily apparent in late spring, when most fields in the thum are lying fallow. Looking across at Banyan Hill from the opposite thum, one can see where the irrigated terraces are scribbled in light green along the river beds and higher up on the hillsides where there are springs. Above these fields and on each side of them are curving bands of orange-red. These are the dry terraces, and they are being plowed at this time of year. In a few places, their solid brick-like color is broken by patches of yellowing wheat not quite ready for harvest.

The Magars of Banyan Hill are subsistence farmers, and the bulk of their food comes from their two kinds of land. Maize and millet are the main dry land crops, with wheat, barley, and dry rice having only secondary importance. The main crop on the irrigated land is, of course, rice. Only occasionally are the paddy fields used for maize.

The climate of the region is monsoonal and subtropical. From the river beds that surround the thum to the ridge above it, the altitude ranges from 2000 feet to only 4000 feet. This combination of climate and relatively low altitude results in a constantly green and tropical lushness, a lushness frequently splotched with brilliant color when flowering trees such as the poinsettia come into bloom. It is a scene of natural, almost jungle-like profusion, but profusion held in check by the careful terracing and the neat farmsteads and paths. One realizes the struggle it took to create a livable niche in these mountains. Yet at the same time, now that the work is finished and all but the most precipitous slopes have been turned into arable fields, one is aware that the worst of the struggle took place long ago; that the heirs to it have found a certain ease.

The deciduous trees that grow everywhere in Banyan Hill and cluster around the houses and line the paths are the source of fodder for livestock. For men and boys one of the daily tasks is to climb these softwoods and strike off their small, sucker-like branches with sickles. Weeds from the terrace walls and from edges of the fields also are used for fodder, together with corn stalks, rice straw, and in certain seasons, a grass that grows on the high open slopes. These high slopes, whose smooth contours are broken in many places by outcroppings of weathered grey stone, provide grazing places for goats and sometimes for cattle and an occasional pony. On the lower hillsides, too, there are a few fairly level places where the soil is too thin for tillage; these also were used for grazing.

Besides the tillage, the deciduous trees that provide fodder, and the open slopes where there is grass and a place for grazing, the other natural feature of major importance for subsistence is forested land where there are hardwoods like the sal tree. One can see the dark green patches that mark these timber stands wherever the river valleys encircling the thum are too steep for terracing but not completely sheer or ledgy.

The basic implements used by the farmers are those that the land suggests: the plow drawn by a yoke of bulls, harrows, drags, mattocks, axes, sickles, and flails. These implements are used in a yearly two-crop seasonal cycle with harvests in the spring and fall.

Sources of Income

There is a saying in Banyan Hill that everyone gets enough to fill his belly. This does not mean that every family obtains enough grain from its own land to meet even its minimum needs. It means rather that if a family does not have a sufficiently large grain income, it can make up the deficit by borrowing or by sending one or more members of the family to work as hired laborers. Actually, there are only seven families whose tillage is so large and productive that they have a saleable surplus. Most other families must purchase grain in amounts varying from more than what is required to support an adult for a year to the very little required to feed a few guests on ceremonial occasions. Even households that are comparatively well off, because they have dry land holdings that are more than adequate, may not have paddy land and must therefore purchase rice. This was true of Indra Kumari. She was fortunate in being able to use surplus millet and maize to obtain rice. Other families, whose dry land holdings were smaller, sometimes had to go into debt to meet their needs for this valued grain. Most people would prefer to sell jewelry rather than suffer the ignominy of having riceless meals for guests.

Since some families need rice and supplemental grain of other kinds, there have to be sources of income other than what the family land can produce. Most families also need an income greater than their land can produce in order to purchase clothing, supplemental butter, cloth, salt, the services of religious specialists, and occasional bazaar items such as powdered color, cigarettes, or a bar of soap.

For most families, trade in livestock provides extra income, even if the sales involve only a few chickens or an occasional buffalo, goat, cow, or pig. A few families sell honey or butter, but the most important local source of income for poorer families is field labor—either for neighboring Brahmans or for wealthier Magars. Bir Bahadur, Dev Bahadur, Lakshmi Devi's son, and a son of Padam Bahadur all worked regularly as plowmen for Brahmans; women like Dubal Singh's wives and Jag Maya frequently went to Brahman farms to grind grain or work in the fields.

The most important nonlocal source of income in Banyan Hill is army service, a source that is part of a long-standing hill tradition. Ever since 1815 Magars, together with Gurungs, Limbus, and Rais, formed the backbone of the British Gurkha Brigade. In the two World Wars half the Nepalese holders of the Victoria Cross, Britain's highest decoration for bravery, were Magars, one of whom came from a village adjacent to Pandera Thum. Hill boys enlisted in their teens, sometimes making their own way to the recruiting depots and sometimes joining a large group that had been banded together by a recruiter. In 1947, at the time of India's independence, the regiments of the Gurkha Brigade were divided, four remaining with the British and six going to India. Nepalese soldiers serving with the British today are mainly in Borneo, Malaya, and Hong Kong, while those serving with the Indians are guarding India's borders with Pakistan and China.

Army service brings additional income to Banyan Hill because there are eight men who served ten years or more in the Gurkha Brigade and now have pensions. Saila Ba, a Subedar, has the largest pension, while Bir Bahadur, who was a Rifleman (a rank comparable to Private) has the smallest. Every year during the winter these men trek to the Indian city of Gorakhpur to collect their money—a trip that may take them, with stops to make purchases, as long as three weeks. Even a small pension is a useful asset, and the larger ones, such as the Subedar's, represent comparative munificence. In Banyan Hill, as elsewhere in the hills, a pensioner like the Subedar holds a position of weight and respect. In large part this is because of his wealth and experience in the larger world, but it also is because he is believed to have been specially favored by the gods and to be affluent because he did good deeds in a previous life.

The Subedar's son, and the son of Tara Maya, his sister, both were serving with the British in Malaya, while Kanchha Ba and Bom Bahadur each had sons serving with the Indians. Most hill boys aspire to get into the British army because the pay and supplemental advantages are considered to be better. Among the most appreciated of fringe benefits is an opportunity for wives to come and live in cantonments in Singapore and Hong Kong.

Income in the form of interest on loans accounts for a high proportion of Banyan Hill's supplemental income. The recipient of most of this money, however, is the Headman, who has been owed as much as 28,000 Nepalese rupees (one U. S. dollar equals 7.6 Nepalese rupees). The other two who had financed the most loans, but on a much smaller scale, were Saila Ba and Kanchha Ba. Although one might expect that Maila Ba also would have financed loans, since he too had an excellent farm, this was not the case. He did not have a pension, and even though he had two wives, he still had to hire farm labor.

The emergency sources of income are jewelry and land, usually in that order. For marginal families, these are the items with which they meet a father's funeral expenses or keep themselves going through a series of bad years. Once the downward spiral of increasing indebtedness has begun, the only way out for many families is a son's enlistment in the army, or the father's finding employment in India. This was true of Padam Bahadur, the most heavily indebted of all Banyan Hill farmers. He had owed 10 percent interest on a loan of Rs 500 for fifteen years. To prevent interest from accruing on a loan of Rs 700, he had sent his son to work for his Brahman creditor who fed the boy. He met the interest on another loan by making a yearly purchase of salt in a distant bazaar and transporting it to his creditor—a transaction that returned interest to the creditor at a rate of 20 percent. All his other large loans were accruing unpaid interest, with the exception of one for Rs 305. In return for this loan, he allowed the creditor to use some of his land and the produce the creditor took from it covered the interest. His troubles began when he had to borrow to pay for the funerals of his father and brother, who died within a week of each other. His financial difficulties were aggravated when two teams of bulls died. Since these misfortunes, his situation had steadily deteriorated. Fortunately, foreclosure is very frequently held in abeyance because creditors foresee the possibility of army service for sons or Indian employment for the father, and they are willing to wait and take their substantial profit in cash rather than in land. This was true of Padam's creditors; during the period when my research was being conducted, his eldest son, despite opposition, did run away and attempt to join the army.

Despite their small pensions, the other farmers who were most heavily in debt were Bir Bahadur, Bom Bahadur, and Dev Bahadur. Bom already had a son in the army, and Bir's son joined Padam's when he made his attempt to enlist. Dev was in the most desperate straits because he had no son who could enlist, and he himself could not go to India because he was the only male in his lineage segment. The only way he could prevent himself from becoming irremediably insolvent was to work as a plowman, and this was not accomplishing the purpose. The advantage of having a son in the army was evident when Kanchha Ba's eldest son returned home on his first leave with savings of Rs 2560, which he turned over to his father.

Purchases

After funerals and similiar emergencies and purchases of livestock and grain, bazaar purchases cause a considerable drain on a family's resources. Butwal is the largest bazaar to which the people of Banyan Hill go regularly, and most pensioners pass this way going to and from Gorakhpur in India. The other large bazaar that attracts trade from Banyan Hill is Pokhara, a town situated on an outwash plain beneath the Annapurna massif two easy days' walk away. Now that it is connected to Kathmandu and other Nepalese towns by air, its drawing power is increasing; it still is less attractive than Butwal because prices are much higher.

The only bazaar of any considerable size that is close to Banyan Hill is a long morning's walk east to the Seti River. Here there are numerous small shops that have been built near a suspension bridge. This bazaar, called Setipul, is especially active on the first day of Magh (January–February) when many people come to the river to take ritual baths. It also attracts trade when hillmen gather for singing contests sponsored by local merchants.

The bazaar most constantly used by the people of Banyan Hill is only a few minutes walk from the hamlet at a trail juncture called Deorali. It is shaded by towering grey-tendoned pipal trees. At one end, the Headman constructed a *dhansar* for travelers—a structure we made our headquarters for the last four months of the research.

The purchase of land, except for very well-to-do families, is rare. Dry land is owned in varying amounts, but every family except Om Bahadur owns some. Paddy land is more valuable and scarce, and there are seven families that have none. As a rule, land that is owned is acquired by inheritance, though small amounts may be acquired in the form of religiously motivated gifts. The custom of financing a loan to obtain the use of a piece of land until the debt is repaid is common. There is also some leasing of land for annual payments of specified amounts of produce, although not necessarily produce grown on the fields themselves. There also is some share-cropping, with the owner usually taking half the crop from the dry land yield and two-thirds from the irrigated land.

The Cultural Context

The culture of Banyan Hill is a result of many influences and a long history. The Tibeto-Burman home language of the Magars points to a place of origin somewhere to the north, in Tibet, South China, or Inner Asia. Nepali, which everyone speaks as a second language, suggests the influence of India and the numerous Brahman neighbors who now are the most important purveyors of this influence. As reminders of a third influence, there are Magar men who are experts in the armament of an infantry battalion, who know that Italians and Chinese eat octopus, and can demonstrate how an Englishman dances. These recall Magar soldiering and contacts far beyond South Asia.

It is difficult to be sure about influences from the north and northeast. When one learns that an essential feature of every Magar marriage is the sacrifice of a chicken, a custom they do not share with the Brahmans, it is tempting to believe that it came with them from another homeland long ago. But one has no assurance that this is true. They could have learned it from indigenous peoples whom they displaced. Magars left their place of origin so long ago that the traces, though surely present, are not as easy to pin down as are the influences from the south and west.

Today Brahmans have been as they have for many centuries, the main source of Indian cultural influence. Brahmans share the Magar claim to be the original inhabitants of Pandera Thum, and they are much more certain of their origins than the Magars. There is no doubt in their minds that originally they came from India. The influences they represent began to be felt in Nepal long before the present era; they seem to have intensified following the eleventh century when Muslim invasions of northern India drove numbers of Brahmans, and members of other Indian castes, into the hills. Among the castes were members of militant ruling groups, such as the Rajputs (called Thakuri in Nepal), and members of the lower artisan castes, such as Metalworkers and Tailors. Racially, many of these people were Caucasoid. Although large numbers of them found homes along the southernmost borders of Nepal, there were many who settled in the middle ranges among tribes such as the Magars—who had themselves originally come from elsewhere. Although the records are scanty and not entirely clear, it seems that some of the refugees, particularly those from groups having a tradition of rule, were able to take over numbers of petty chiefdoms that already existed under the leadership of local rulers. At any rate, over the course of time there was much racial mixing of these outsiders and such local Tibeto-Burman-speaking peoples as the Magars; this is readily apparent in many Magar faces and even in the faces of many who claim unmixed descent from ruling houses of India.

Cultural Processes

Since the mixed culture of Banyan Hill and its echo in the mixed racial stocks is the product of a long historical development, it is impossible now to unravel many of the specific aspects of this history. But many of the same processes are at work today that were present in the past, and one can readily see how they reflect the geography of Nepal.

One of the best ways to see such processes is to set out on one of the paths leading away from Banyan Hill down into the steep river valley to the west. Following this valley, the path winds south through paddy fields to a junction with a larger stream. It then crosses a ridge and drops down to Kalipar on the Kali Gandaki River. The trip takes about five hours. At Kalipar there is a small collection of hostels, a ferry consisting of a dugout canoe, and a temple complex. This is a place where people from a wide area, including Banyan Hill, come to float their dead down the river or to bury or cremate them. It is where they come to secure the services of a Brahman priest or to bathe on occasions of special religious significance in the Hindu calendar. It is an important ferry point because the path on the other side leads south to Butwal and India.

In past eons, the Kali Gandaki River sliced its way through the highest ridge of the Himalayas and created the immense gorge between the Dhaulagiri and Annapurna massifs. As similar rivers that have breached the great mountain wall have, the Kali has provided a fairly easy passage for people and influences from the north. It also is one of the pathways to India, but more important than this—since many other trails are available—it provides sites from which Indian culture can be disseminated. Like the Ganges, of which it is a tributary, it becomes one of the holy rivers of Hinduism, and all along its banks one can find Hindu temples with dedicated Hindus in attendance. At Kalipar, the focus of religious life is a hill Brahman who studied many years in Banaras, became a follower of Vishnu, and has had a strong effect on many people in the surrounding region.

As ferry point, path juncture, and Hindu religious center, a day in Kalipar during the fall of the year provides suggestive evidence of the extent and kinds of historical contact that the people of Banyan Hill have had with the culture areas of the north and south, as well as evidence of its contemporary contact not only with these areas but also with other regions of Asia and with Europe.

Early in the day, a boatload of men and women from India are ferried across. They are accompanied by porters and are on their way to visit Muktinath, a famous Hindu shrine at one of the sources of the Kali Gandaki near the Tibetan border. They are accompanied by an Indian holy man who will leave the group and spend some months begging in hill villages on his way south, telling not only about the Hindu center at Muktinath but also about marvels imputed to relics in one of the nearby Buddhist shrines. After making the crossing, the pilgrims stop for tea at a hostel near the Kalipar temple. The hostel consists of a temporary shelter made of brush and matting. The proprietor and his wife are members of a group whose permanent homes are in towns along the river beyond the highest Himalayan ranges not far from Muktinath. These people, called Thakalis, fan out everywhere in the Kali Gandaki drainage during the winter months to operate these small trailside hostels, and as a sideline, to trade in horses and in any other kind of commodity with which they can turn a small profit. Although touched by Hinduism, these people are predominantly Buddhist in their beliefs and practices. Later in the day, one sees further evidence of northern culture and Buddhism when a Tibetan curer stops here and recites Tibetan spells over a patient while singing a Tibetan tune. A number of travelers who cross the river are ex-soldiers traveling south, often with their wives, to collect their pensions and spend some of it for cloth, spices, salt, jewelry, and trinkets. Many of the older men served in the Middle East or France in the First World War, and many fought in the Second World War and served in Burma, North Africa, or Italy. One generally can tell a pensioner because he will be wearing some item of his old uniform. This sets him apart from another kind of traveler, the village men and women carrying heavily loaded wicker baskets with tump lines. They come from northwest of Banyan Hill and are carrying butter in kerosene tins or in black wooden jars. They will sell the butter in the important southern border town and trade center, Butwal. Added to all these people, at one time or another during the day, there are a miscellaneous variety of other travelers: a Brahman priest going to participate as a reader of Sanskrit in a seven-day ceremony; a groom and his party going to pick up a bride; a villager going to a cattle fair to buy a calf; a group of boys and girls on their way to spend a night singing in a nearby bazaar town; a spruce young soldier in shorts and army boots home on his first leave from Malaya; a litigant on the way to the district court; a heavily loaded group of brass sellers who have made the eleven days' walk from Kathmandu, the capital and major city in Nepal; two professional hill minstrels going to beg and sing around the Indian industrial complex at Jamshedpur. They arrive at Kalipar at dusk and in return for liquor or food, they play and sing for their fellow travelers. Their repertoire includes stories about famous figures in Nepalese history, recent events such as the ascent of Everest, love songs, hymns to Hindu gods, humorous songs, and Indian cinema songs.

In its essential outlines, the movement of people seen at this river crossing can be found at other river crossings throughout the southerly reaches of Central Nepal; although such movement exists in somewhat diminished form elsewhere throughout the country, it is here along these natural arteries that the movement of peoples and ideas is most intense. Despite the fact that almost all movement is on foot, Nepal is a land of travelers; ideas from its immediate borders and some too from Southeast Asia, the Middle East, and Europe continually flow into the country and are spread from region to region. In this fashion, Nepalese culture becomes a medley of different strands with shadings of intensity toward Tibet in the north and India in the south.

Yet it is not enough to say that Nepalese culture and the variant of it represented in Banyan Hill is a series of separate elements. Actually it is more truly described as a blend in which separate elements still are discernible but are altered because they exist as parts of a new combination. The Nepalese caste system is an example. In India, a marriage across caste lines usually brings severe sanctions. In Nepal the rule of caste endogamy has been relaxed and one finds Brahmans who have married Magar women or, as in Banyan Hill, a Magar woman who has married an Ex-Slave. These marriages are not regarded as the most desirable, but they are condoned. The existence of this blending, with its unique Nepalese tincture, reminds one that despite rivers and paths and a surprisingly mobile population, Nepal is one of the most mountainous countries in the world. People travel, but travel is not easy. There are no bridges over long stretches of many rivers, and they become impassable during the summer months of monsoon rains. Even when the water is low, there are many fords where it is safest to wait for another traveler on the proven theory that four feet on slippery rocks are safer than two. Frail bridges frequently become unsafe and landslides sweep away trails. Thus, while it is true that communities like Banyan Hill are permeable from the outside, and have always received new ideas, they are still mountain communities. Influences from the outside, though not stopped, are slowed and weakened and become more amenable to the stamp of the hillmen's special needs and character.

The Nation

The Kali Gandaki may be used to symbolize and partly explain the cultural and racial mixture of north and south. But if the people of Banyan Hill follow patterns of life that reflect India, and Central Asia and Tibet, and even to some slight degree, Europe, they also live in a cultural and social milieu that is national. They never think of themselves as a combination of elements or as a blend. But in some contexts they do think of themselves as Nepalese, and the fact that this is so, not only in Banyan Hill but from one end of the kingdom of Nepal to the other, is largely the result of the movement toward unification begun in the eighteenth century by Prithivi Narayan Sah and continued by his heirs.

Prithivi Narayan was a hill chieftain who claimed Rajput status. He came from a small village called Gorkha in the center of Nepal. Prior to his rise—a rise based on his drive and organizing genius and on the rifles with which he was able to equip his troops—Nepal consisted of a patchwork of petty chiefdoms and their shifting alliances. By the end of the eighteenth century, Prithivi Narayan and his relatives in the House of Gorkha had unified the country and laid the administrative, legal, and military foundations of the present national structure. Unity was fostered by the spread of Nepali, the Sanskrit-derived dialect also spoken by the chiefs of Gorkha and numbers of their troops and administrative officers. The language gradually became the *lingua franca* for the whole country. The subsequent kings of Nepal, who always were scions of the House of Gorkha, provided the capstone symbol of nationhood. In time, they came to be regarded as living gods and today when the present king walks in the hills many people gather up dust from places in the path where he has stepped. This reverence for the king has done much to hold the disparate people of Nepal together as a nation. Equally important was the fact that although the national government had power enough to strike down rebellion, it generally did not have enough to make centralized rule onerous. People in Banyan Hill pay taxes, but within an unburdensome structure that has undergone little change for over a century.

The national government is represented in Banyan Hill by two revenue officials (*Jimuals*), who collect taxes on irrigated land, and by eight official headmen (*Mukhiyas*), who collect taxes on dry land. The *Mukhiyas* are the usual channel through which the government makes contact with the village, and they are expected to keep order. The district headquarters is in Nuwakot where jail, court, and tax office are situated on a high hill about two days' easy walk or one day's hard walk from Banyan Hill. Kathmandu, where the central government is located and the king has his palace, used to be ten hard days on foot from Banyan Hill. Now it can be reached by walking to Pokhara and flying for forty-five minutes; a trip that a number of people in Pandera Thum have made, including the Banyan Hill headman and four of his sons.

Gustatory Godlings

Gods and Godlings

As ONE WALKS along the trails and paths of Banyan Hill one notices—beside a path, beneath a tree, under a large stone, beside a spring—little rectangular pieces of cowdung, on a platform, with a varying number of evenly spaced depressions in the top, such as might be made with the tip of a finger. Sometimes these platforms are uncovered, resting on a patch of earth that has been hardened and made smooth with a mixture of mud, cowdung, and water. But most of them are inside little "rooms" that are open in front and have been made with flat stones. On occasion, too, one sees a small pavilion with a conical thatched roof made of straw, about the height of a man. These are some of the places where one can make contact with supernatural beings of a particular kind—the beings who mean most to the majority of people in Banyan Hill, because they are the ones who are effective in their lives and really make a difference. Although they generally are worshipped on the home terrain of Nepal and thought of as being part of that familiar landscape, the power of some of them reaches as far as distant European or Asian army camps or battlefields. Coming to terms with these beings is a part of what most people believe they must do to stay alive and well. These are beings of the land and of the forces controlling health, growth, and reproduction. Meeting their demands—which is actually "feeding" them—is as necessary for the continuation of life as is feeding one's buffaloes with fodder or the soil with manure.

These beings, who may be either male (*devta*) or female (*devi*), are referred to as deities who eat food or *bhog*. *Bhog* is a word that connotes more than mere food. It connotes the pleasure of eating, and sensual pleasures generally. Hence the phrase by which these beings are referred to, *bhog-khanne-devta* (or *devi*), means gods (or goddesses) who eat with relish and pleasure; what they enjoy most is the newly spilled blood of a sacrificial animal.

For the Vaishnavites of Banyan Hill there is a clear distinction between beings who demand live sacrifice and those who do not. The latter, such as Vishnu, are sometimes referred to as incense-eating gods or goddesses, *dhup-khanne-devta* or *devi*. They are said to be in heaven and to like food that rises up like smoke rather than falling to the ground like blood. Although the Magars of Banyan Hill refer to some of both kinds of supernatural by the word *devta* or *devi,* we will use god or goddess for deities who prefer incense and godlings for those who prefer blood.

Vaishnavites do not worship the godlings at all. They believe that Vishnu in all his forms is so powerful that there is no need to turn elsewhere for help and protection. Non-Vaishnavite Brahmans believe it is appropriate to worship certain manifestations of Shiva with live sacrifice, but they would not worship Vishnu in this way. Magars are less clear about the distinction between gods and goddesses and godlings. The Havildar Major, who is typical of most Magars in the area, worships Lakshmi, the consort of Vishnu, by sacrificing a hen. The whole ceremony is very little different from his worship of the Hunter Godling in Maila Ba's field. It is an example of how Magars tend to draw supernatural beings that Brahmans define as gods and goddesses into a godling pattern.

Perhaps this is because the gods and goddesses are somewhat bodiless and abstract to most Magars. They are far away in heaven, a place that is less real than the surrounding countryside where the godlings live. In a vague way, gods and goddesses tend the world and do good; on appropriate occasions, such as a naming ceremony or a funeral, they must be reached by Sanskrit prayers and the Brahman's ritual fire. But it is the godlings who most often cause evil, just as it is they who give protection during war, bring about a promotion, cure the sick child, make the buffalo fertile, and keep borers out of the maize.

The godlings present a bewildering welter of characteristics, but there are a number of generalizations that can be applied. All are capable of good and evil, and it would be hard to find any evil that some one of them at some time had not brought about. But there is some tendency to specialize, and some godlings specialize in frustrating (or forwarding) the agricultural enterprise. One is the tiger that carries off livestock, another the crow that pulls up the sprouting maize, and a third the spirit-source of the buffalo's miscarriage.

Godlings do not expect much, but they are sensitive to slight and become angry and spiteful when they are not given their due. With few exceptions, all godlings expect food at regular intervals. There is one time of year especially when families believe they should make an offering to a number of them. This is the time of the spring full moon. Any full moon period is called *purne;* as this one usually falls in the lunar month of Baisakh (April–May), it is referred to as Baisakh *purne.* In 1961 it fell on April 30.

Godlings who have been regularly propitiated still may cause trouble. When misfortune occurs, the family generally sends for one of the two specialists who can determine whether a godling is the cause, and if so, which godling and what will be required to appease him. One specialist is the astrologer. Astrologers belong to the Jaisi Brahman caste, a type of Brahman that results when an Upadhyaya Brahman—the highest ranking Brahman in this part of Nepal—

marries a Brahman widow. These Brahmans cannot conduct Vedic rites but are mostly literate and function as part-time astrologers. Mainly they determine causes of misfortune by consulting astrological tables. The other specialist is the shaman. These men can be members of any caste, though in Pandera Thum the best known shaman is a Magar. A shaman has a variety of ways of determining causes of evil, but the skill that defines him professionally is the ability to call godlings, to become possessed by them, and to permit them to speak through his mouth.

Occasionally an individual discovers the cause of the trouble in a dream. A godling may come to him, say why he is causing trouble and tell what he requires if he is to be persuaded to stop. Should the astrologer or shaman say that a godling the family has been propitiating regularly is angry, a reason may or may not be given. Baseless anger is characteristic of godlings. But their desires generally are definite, and for the majority of them, chicken blood is what is most wanted.

Method of Sacrifice

Sacrifices (pujas) are made at places where is it believed the godling lives. The sacrifices almost always are made by a young, unmarried boy, called a *pujari*, who bathes and puts on a clean white loin cloth, which is the only clothing he wears. After cleaning the ground with cowdung and water, thus setting it apart and making it acceptable for a holy purpose, he winds string around a stone and sets it upright to represent the godling being honored. The string represents the godling's new clothing. The basic rationale throughout the puja is doing things for the godling that will be pleasing: clothing him, feeding him, and surrounding him with pleasant things like incense and flowers. It is equally important to do these things in a properly sanctified place, with the ritual conducted by a person who has prepared himself by bathing and who has not yet lost the extra purity believed to belong to the unmarried. This latter quality is especially important to female godlings but is appreciated by the males as well.

After making a cowdung platform for food offerings and setting it before the stone, the *pujari* decorates the shrine with tumeric, rice flour, bits of colored cloth, and flowers. Offerings that are then placed in the holes of the cowdung platform include rice flour fried in butter, puffed rice, rice mixed with water and sage, and cow's milk. The godling also is honored by offerings of flowers and by the presence of fire in the form of a mustard oil lamp in a copper container.

Just before the sacrifice, the *pujari* makes an incense of butter and sage and prays for whatever boon he wishes, pointing out that he is about to offer a sacrifice. The animal to be offered is sanctified by putting water, rice, and sage on its head until it nods its willingness to be killed. Then it is waved in the incense and beheaded. The head is placed before the stone and the blood is spurted about on the shrine. After the sacrifice, the *pujari* gives *tikka* by pressing small amounts of a mixture of rice and sacrificial blood onto the foreheads of those who are present. He receives tikka by having one of the worshippers do the same for him. As a gift for his services, he gets the head of the sacrificed animal and whatever food has been brought as an offering. The final act of the puja is cooking and eating the sacrificed animal that now has been shared with the godling.

This type of ceremony also is performed by the Brahmans in Pandera Thum, and the Brahmans honor almost all the same godlings as the Magars do. There are some differences, though, in the way they worship them. Any Brahman, for example, married or unmarried, can act as *pujari*. Brahmans chant verses in Sanskrit (from the *Yajur Veda*) and do not offer any tumeric; unlike most Magars, they insist on barley, sesame, dharba grass, and sandalwood paste— elements that figure in all pujas that are done by the local Brahmans. Also, where Magars frequently conduct their ceremonies communally, Brahmans always do them as a domestic ritual. The Brahman ceremony, in brief, contains all the elements of a simple Hindu puja. The Magar ceremony, while clearly modeled on it garbles some elements, omits others, and adds live sacrifice.

Hunter Godling and Sansari Mai

Godlings as a rule cannot be seen. They make themselves known through what they do, or fail to do; the closest approach to a physical realization of their presence is in dreams or at the sites where it is believed they live. But there is one godling who does appear in person with some frequency, and who even has been visited at his places of residence. This is the Hunter Godling. Actually, although the conception always is similar, there are a number of manifestations of the Hunter Godling, and it would be more correct to speak of Hunter Godlings in the plural. The two most commonly mentioned Hunter Godlings in Banyan Hill are Suno, who has blond hair and is a small boy, and Rithe, who has dark hair and is more like an adult man. Suno (meaning gold) and Rithe (meaning black) are similar in most other respects. Their hair is said to have a tendency to point forward, whereas a normal human's hair is thought to have a tendency to lie back. Both are hunters, and in addition to live sacrifice and the usual puja, they like to have a gift of a miniature bow and quiver. Both have wives, and sometimes the wives are given miniature combs, baskets, tump lines, and bows for shooting small stones and clay pellets. Unlike their husbands, the wives cause no one any trouble. An offering to them is a courtesy. The Hunter Godlings have dogs, which they use for the chase, and at night men have heard the ringing of the bells they wear. The Hunter Godlings are mainly associated with cattle disease, but they also can cause human illness and have an influence on crops.

Any Hunter Godling, it is believed, can spirit people away to the place where he lives, usually thought to be a cave. In the vicinity of Banyan Hill, two men at different times were taken away by Hunter Godlings, one by Suno, the other by Rithe. One was a Brahman with a withered arm and the other was an Ex-Slave. The Ex-Slave was kept away for three days, the Brahman for four. In the case of the Brahman, whose experience closely paralleled the Ex-Slave's, he was taken to the godling's cave and made to study esoteric lore having to do with control of spirits. The godling's cook was said to be Black Bhairam, a manifestation of Shiva, and was told to beat the Brahman when he did not apply himself assiduously to his studies. Rice, cooked in milk and containing almonds and spices, was served on a golden plate, and no matter how much was eaten, the portion never diminished. At the end of the period, both men found themselves back at their homes, with no memory of how they had arrived there. Although neither of them became shamans as a result of this experience, nor were there any men around Banyan Hill who had, it was said that other men who had remained with Hunter Godlings from four to six months had learned a great deal and were exceptionally skillful.

Some godlings affect only single families, or just a few families. These godlings, such as the Household Godling, will be discussed in the chapter on family. All the others can affect many families. Any one of them *can* be worshipped by a single family and many, such as the Hunter Godling, usually are. But any of these godlings also can be worshipped by a neighborhood group—a group that often crosses caste lines. Maila Ba, Saila Ba, Havildar Major, and a neighboring Ex-Slave, and a Metalworker together worship a Hunter Godling in Maila Ba's field, with Havildar Major's son acting as *pujari*. Havildar Major believes the godling is Suno. Logically he could worship this godling with another family, at another place. It is partly convenience that brings him to join Maila Ba. However, the more important reason is the fact that an astrologer told Saila Ba that a Hunter Godling who lived in Maila Ba's fields was causing his goats to die, information that made it seem only sensible to the Havildar to try and keep on this godlings's good side. The problem of whether it really is Suno or whether it might be Rithe, and whether whichever godling it is might be just as well pleased with an offering made elsewhere, is not regarded as a significant problem.

Some godlings are not worshipped regularly but only when they cause trouble. Sansari Mai, a female godling who causes cattle disease, falls into this category. When she was worshipped, the puja generally was communal, as cattle disease easily could become epidemic. In a neighboring hamlet when cattle disease struck, there were thirty-two houses that contributed to her worship. Each house sent leaf plates containing butter, unhulled and hulled rice, white string, rice flour and tumeric, and strips of either white or red cloth. Each also contributed money to purchase a black goat, and eleven houses each contributed a chicken. Nine men and a few children were present during the proceedings. After the goat had been sacrificed, it was singed, and some of the men divided it up into thirty-two portions. These were wrapped up in banana leaves, and the men dropped off a single portion at each of the participating houses. Most of the sacrificed chickens also were returned to the houses that sent them, but some of the people who attended the ceremony had brought extra rice so that they could cook their mid-morning meal at the shrine. They also cooked their sacrificed chicken and turned the occasion into a picnic.

Promises

Godlings have varying degrees of power. Although all godlings attract "promises" of worship for specific boons, it is those with a reputation for exceptional power who attract the most. A common occasion for promising a puja to such a godling is when someone in the family is ill. If a child is sick, the father goes to the spring, takes a bath, and puts on clean clothing. When he comes home, he makes a leaf plate and puts some rice in it, along with a copper *pice*. The pice, a small coin, stands for Shiva, who becomes a witness to the promise. The father touches the child with the leaf plate and says, taking the name of the godling he wishes to call on for help, "Please trouble this child no more, and I will do a puja for you." The plate and its contents are hidden away somewhere in the house, usually between the top of the wall and the roof. It cannot be touched until the puja has been done and serves as a reminder of the promise. One reason it is difficult to get chickens to eat when trekking in Nepal is because so many of them have been promised to godlings and are being saved for sacrifice on a specific date.

Some potentially beneficient godlings attract more promises than others. One shrine in the village, a large stone structure under an ancient banyan tree, is the home of Grandmother Godling Satiwanti. It is in a stone enclosure and at the back of the enclosure is another small shrine, said to be the home of her teacher, or *guru,* a woman who belongs to the Leatherworker caste. Leatherworkers are Untouchable, and after worshipping here the *pujari* must have water sprinkled on him by a member of a clean caste so as to remove the pollution of contact. During the Burma campaign, in which he served, Dev Bahadur promised, if his life was spared, to sacrifice five chickens, and to commemorate the sacrifice both with a carved post to be set up outside the shrine, and with a bell to be hung inside it. He did this promptly on his safe return from the war. Such a sacrifice of five living things commemorated by a carved post and a bell frequently is promised by soldiers.

Both shrines where the most promises are made are a half day's hard walk away, one to the west, the other to the east. One is sacred to Black Bhairam. It consists of an unroofed, stone-walled enclosure large enough to hold two or three men, and is spectacularly situated at the top of a very high barren hill. The central image is a smooth black stone. Promises can be made to Bhairam for anything one wishes—a son, a wife, a promotion, good crops, destruction of an enemy. The sacrifice of five live things is common. The carved pole commemorating the sacrifice must be topped by a trident, symbol of Shiva. Bells are given also, and in addition bamboo poles decorated with cloth. A portion of the shrine is packed with these memorials. At this shrine the *pujari* is traditionally a Magar and he is supported by portions of the sacrifices and by income from land which has been given for the shrine's support.

The second shrine has a slightly different aura. It is in the woods on a hillside where there is a spring that alternately flows copiously, filling up a small stone-lined tank, and stops flowing, permitting the tank to drain. This shrine also is supported by a grant of land, but the traditional attendant is a Brahman. The shrine is sacred to Barahi, a manifestation of Shiva's consort. The boons that can be asked are the same as those that can be asked of Bhairam, including the destruction of enemies. The same animal sacrifices can be made, except that pigs are not appropriate here. Nearby on the hillside above the shrine there is a small religious retreat in charge of an elderly woman, who had dedicated her life to Shiva. Visitors to the shrine frequently come to her hut to pay their respects. At both shrines many of the bells are inscribed. A high proportion of them have been donated by soldiers, especially at the shrine of Black Bhairam.

Origins

Some godlings originate in the hamlet itself as transformed human beings. A godling worshipped by Bir Bahadur, Havildar Santa Prasad, and some Metalworkers in their locality is a *mari*. She came into existence when a woman died in childbirth. The *mari* is worshipped at the place where her house used to stand. Most persons, including men, who die violent deaths become *mari*. The exceptions are soldiers who die in battle. They do not join the earthbound, frequently dissatisfied or angry godlings, but they go immediately to be among their ancestors in heaven.

The godling pantheon is dynamic and flexible, with some godlings being added as others are forgotten; more than anyone else, the shamans are the ones who keep people informed of its changing and locally relevant dimensions. One could see how the process had occurred in a hamlet adjacent to Banyan Hill. Here a shaman discovered that a godling had begun to affect the people of the community. She was called the Three River Godling and had been born to the east of Pandera Thum where there was a confluence of three rivers. The shaman was treating a sick man, and when he fell into a state of possession, the Three River Godling spoke through his mouth and said, "Yes, I am giving him this illness. I am in a stone at the edge of Dev Bahadur's rice field. The stone is marked with three clefts. Bring the stone to Sikha and build a temple. Every three years all you people must sacrifice five living things there. On intervening years you must sacrifice at least a cock and a goat. Whenever these sacrifices are made the Tailors must be called to play on their instruments and dance."

The shaman and others went to the field and found the stone. It was brought to a place near the village where a number of paths cross, and a small building of wattle and daub and thatch was built over it. The man recovered, and for twelve years the people of the village have been making yearly sacrifices. The godling also asked the people to light an oil lamp in the temple at sunset of the night following the sacrifices; she wanted people, young people especially, to play in the vicinity and sing all night. This also the people do. On the occasion of the yearly sacrifices, villagers bring rice. Part is used to pay the *pujari* and part is used to pay the Tailor musicians. The people of Sikha also bring the first fruits of their maize harvest, and no one eats maize until the *pujari* has made a collective offering of it at the temple. By following her requests, the people of Sikha believe that the Three River Godling has protected the village from serious farming losses and from the ravages of serious epidemics.

This addition to the local pantheon has had wide effects, especially on the Sikha community. But there are additions to the pantheon that affect only a few families. Hem Bahadur, the husband of Sita Devi, had a dream when he was in Shillong. He dreamed a godling called Singha Devi came to him and told him she was living behind his mother's house, beside a tree. When he came back from Assam he fell ill. He himself was a shaman, and during the course of his illness he held a séance and became possessed by Singha Devi, who told him that if he did puja to her at the place where she was living, he would be cured. The next day he went to the place, did puja, and soon afterwards he recovered. Since that time, about fifteen years ago, all the Darkang families have been making offerings at this shrine every month on the fifth day after the new moon. Persons in Darkang who get sore eyes cure them by taking a flower and offering it to Singha Devi. As yet there have been no persons outside of this group who have worshipped her. But if a shaman were to find that she was troubling others, they too would begin to make offerings.

Magar Godlings

There are three godlings of great importance who are believed to have begun their existence long ago as Magars. Besides whatever individual or family offerings are made, both always are worshipped communally. Two who always are worshipped together are conceived of as one and are referred to as Grandfather-Grandmother. Their puja is given in the month of Mangsir (November—December), when two pigs generally are sacrificed. They are regarded as powerful witches and cause more anxiety than most godlings, especially at night, when people prefer not to mention them.

Grandfather and Grandmother once were a Magar man and his wife, and at that time, too, both were thought to be witches. They lived with their son, his wife and their two little grandsons. During the day the son and his wife used to go to work in the fields, leaving the children at home with the grandparents. The mother, however, used to come back from time to time to suckle the children, and she noticed that they usually were crying as if in pain. She became suspicious and suggested that instead of going to the fields, she and her husband should conceal themselves near the house and see what happened. When they did this they saw the old couple taking the hearts and livers from the children's bodies and eating them. Afterwards, they hung the bodies of the children on the fence that surrounded the courtyard. Later, when the old couple expected the mother and father to return, they brought the children back to life. When the parents saw what was happening and knew that the grandfather and grandmother were witches, they put the grandfather into a large clay pot and the grandmother into a skin bag. After burying the grandfather beside the river, they tossed the grand-mother in and let her float off. The people around Banyan Hill believe that the old people reappeared together at a place called Diskinkot. Their arrival was marked by a severe epidemic. Now they wander throughout Nepal and whenever their influence is felt people or their cattle fall ill from a variety of diseases.

Appropriately, the puja to Grandfather-Grandmother is one of the few that does not follow the pattern of worship described earlier. It is more like the ceremony used for ancestor worship by Magars who do not call a Brahman for this purpose. Except for the festival of Dasain, the Grandfather-Grandmother puja is the occasion on which Magar relatives do the most visiting.

The third Magar godling is Mandale. He began life as a human, and many say that Grandfather and Grandmother were his maternal uncle and aunt. One day Mandale's wife said, "I would like to eat some pork." He replied, "I will go get a pig." He took some rice and said a spell over it. He gave it to his wife and said, "When I come back I will come as a tiger and be bringing a pig. Throw this rice on me and I will become myself again, and we can eat the pig." But when he came back as a tiger his wife was so frightened she forgot what to do and ran in-side the house. From then on Mandale has remained a tiger.

Mandale is worshipped every month, with each household being attached to one of the various shrines giving rice and other items necessary for carrying out a puja. Once a year in Mangsir (November–December) a cooperative puja is done in which Mandale is offered a pig. When Mandale is propitiated fully and correctly, it is believed that tigers, all of whom are manifestations of his spirit, will not eat the people of the village or their cattle.

Household Godling

Each family has a godling whose effects are limited to that family alone. This is the Household Godling, a male godling who comes to reside in the kitch-en-room whenever a new house is built. It is the only godling to be honored with live sacrifice within the house. He looks to the well-being of the household mem-bers, their cattle, and their crops and is worshipped once a year in the month of Jeth (May–June). The eldest living male in the family is officiant at the puja, and the usual sacrifice is a cock that has been promised at the ceremony the year before. The puja is done in the kitchen-room at the back. There is a morning and an evening phase, both of which are very much the same, except that no live sacrifice is made at night. In the morning half, nine leaf plates containing both rice and a piece of the yeast used for causing fermentation in beer are offered. Beside them another leaf plate containing the same substances is offered to his religious adviser (*guru*) or, some say, to his porter. Then the yearling cock, al-ways referred to as the "old cock," is sacrificed. Before he is killed, he is placed beside the small chick that is to be given the following year and a leaf is rubbed three times down his neck and onto the chick, transferring the promise. Should the small chick turn out to be a hen, she and all her chicks will be offered, and none of her eggs will be eaten. In the puja made by Maila Ba, he said the following prayer before offering the cock: "I am remembering you every year. Please take care of my family." No meat of the old cock can be transported beyond the confines of the farmstead, nor can any of it be eaten by anyone not a member of the lineage. An uncle, for example, may invite his brother's sons to come and eat some of it, and he could also invite their unmarried sisters. Their married sisters would be excluded because they are regarded as members of their husbands' lineages.

The gustatory godlings are emblems of two ideas: the idea of reciprocity and the idea of scarcity. Both ideas are central to the culture and society of Banyan Hill. In the functioning of the society, marriage is a focal working out of the idea of reciprocity. Each family gives daughters in marriage and expects ritual services in return. It also receives wives for its sons and becomes obligated to provide the same services it receives. The idea of scarcity is evident here as it is everywhere. Women are scarce, and valuable; so is land, forest, water, grass, food. In the minds of the Magars of Banyan Hill, anything one has is valuable, both in the sense that it is in short supply and in the sense that in receiving it someone has been deprived. This is true of life itself, and health. The godlings express the inevitable ambiguities of such a situation.

Godlings can be good. They give, just as humans give. The Hunter Godling and Mandale, the tiger, have given up their forests so the land can be terraced. Grandfather-Grandmother, who are prototypes of all ancestors, by their deaths have relinquished claims to an estate their descendants now enjoy. *Mari*, the spirit of those who suffered violent death, has had its life wrested away and its lost life is the life the living now enjoy.

The godlings are gustatory because in this land where life is so precarious and the means of life so difficult to secure, there is no conception of endless bounty and painless giving. The godlings express the idea that to receive is to deprive, to give is to be "taken." That is why they can be both good and evil. They are evil because they hunger for what they have given; since in the final analysis what they give is life, the only fitting return is live sacrifice. Whether it is land, crops, water, fertility in animals, or health, the ultimate meaning to the Magars of the gustatory godlings and their blood-spattered shrines is that one pays with death for the gift of life.

4

Family: Farmstead, Marriage, Husband and Wife

Farmstead

THE CENTER of family life is the farmstead. Some of the Banyan Hill farmsteads are like little islands. They are approached by a lane from a major path, often with a pole gate at the entrance, and surrounded by fences and tall shade trees. Other farmsteads belonging to poorer families are built closer together; by placing the houses so that the doors do not face each other, even they remain separate and distinct. The farmstead-households are the focal units in Banyan Hill society and their isolation serves to accent their importance.

The walls of the houses are built of stones and mud mortar and are smoothly plastered inside and out with a mixture of mud and cowdung. Roofs are thatched and each house has a verandah. The main room has a firepit at one end, and in the wall next to it there is a small, latticed window opening onto the verandah. A narrow strip of floor space at the other end of the room opposite the window and firepit is sacred to the Household Godling, and in many houses this is where offerings to the ancestors are made. Most of the household's grain and valuables are stored in the single upper-storey room, a place kept crisply dry by smoke from the fire below. Essentially the very dark and smoky Magar house is a storeroom, shrine, cooking and eating place. Sometimes during cold or very wet weather, it also is used for sleeping, and the family range themselves around the firepit. Usually, though, people find places to sleep outside, on the verandahs or in some of the outbuildings.

Whatever outbuildings there are will be arranged roughly in a circle, so that they define a courtyard area. It is the courtyard, plus the verandahs and the open-sided *dhansars,* that are the focus for Magar home life. The courtyard is the scene of marriage ceremonies, the performance of a shaman or a dance group;

spectators who are not sitting in the courtyard itself find places on the verandah or in the second storey of the *dhansar*. Dishes are washed on a stone at its far end, and the courtyard is the threshing floor for barley, wheat heads, and pulse. When stored grain is to be dried, it is spread here on large finely woven bamboo mats, guarded by the woman of the house who uses a long thin bamboo pole to keep the chickens away. It is the playground for children and the new goat, the open air workshop for making a basket or a new plowshare, and the domain every year, for one year, of the rooster kept for sacrifice to the Household Godling.

Selecting Brides

In Banyan Hill most families consist only of father, mother, and unmarried children, or some truncated version of this nuclear type. Such families begin with the marriage of a couple, or soon thereafter. First marriages almost always are arranged by the parents, especially when the marriage is the first for both the boy and the girl. The boy and girl can be married at a very early age. The girl may be only nine and the boy twelve. But as a rule the boy is over fifteen and the girl at least twelve or thirteen. Sometimes a young man who is personally unattractive and comes from a poor family may have to wait until his thirty's to find a wife. On the other hand, girls from a prominent and well-to-do family sometimes reach their twenty's before they are married because the local young men and their families do not regard themselves as eligible to ask for an alliance.

There was a similar but more complicated situation in Admara, a community adjacent to Banyan Hill. Here the man who used to be an official headman, and still retained much of the aura of office (a status he actually had lost in a political joust with the headman of Banyan Hill) had three daughters who attracted admirers but had never married. Since two of them were well beyond an age when most local girls married, the situation was the subject of much speculation and gossip. The difficulty seemed to be that the ex-headman's prestige, or in village terms, his "name," was much greater than his wealth. His name tended to scare off poorer suitors, while his actual economic status tended to scare off those who were well-to-do.

A very young boy or a very young girl may not see their spouse-to-be until the wedding occurs. All arrangements will have been made without consulting them. When the children are older, they are more apt to be consulted, and chances are they have seen and perhaps talked with their partner.

If there is to be a formal marriage ceremony and the bride is a virgin girl, the engagement is solemnized with relatives and friends. The groom brings a gift of food to the bride's people. The most important element in this gift is curd. If the elder who represents the bride's father and mother and the brothers of the father accept the curd, the marriage is regarded as legally consummated. Should the arrangements then be broken off for any reason, the bridegroom-to-be is in a position legally to collect compensation. Technically the girl would be known as *jari*, a once married girl who has left her husband and gone to another man.

There are girls who lose their virginity to boys, but it happens clandestinely. If pregnancy does not result, the only notice taken by the community is gossip. But when it happens openly, pressures to define the union as a marriage come into existence. Occasionally a boy and a girl may run away together. If the boy is living alone, as Dhem Bahadur was, they would go to his house. From a strictly legal point of view, even if the girl were not pregnant, such a couple would be considered to be married, because there is presumption of physical contact. From a local point of view, since all the necessary *ceremonial* elements of a marriage are not present, the girl could run away again in a day or two with another boy and her "husband" could not collect compensation. Nevertheless because of the open nature of the act, people would consider the girl to have lost her virginity, and ritually her status could be somewhat compromised. This could appear when she cooked black pulse and a porridge made of millet flour. Both these foods are considered dangerous, probably because they are black and are associated with Yama, the judge of the underworld, and because black pulse is used in the funeral rites. For many Magars, their preparation and consumption are hedged with taboos. Magars who are strict about such things will not take black pulse or millet flour from the kitchen of another Magar unless a number of conditions have been met. The cook must have been married as a virgin. When the foods are cooked, the floor around the kitchen fire should be made ritually pure with a mixture of cowdung, mud, and water. The cook should bathe in water that is ritually pure (that is, water that has been drawn from a stream or well, with none of it poured away for a purpose other than the one at hand), and he should put on clean clothing. During the cooking, the woman should not leave the fireplace, and she should remain there while the food is being eaten. There are some Magars who would not accept these foods from the kitchen of a girl who had run away and lived with a man. This holds even though according to local custom her "husband" could not claim she had married him (so long as they had no children and the union did not last too long), and even though she subsequently might have the kind of marriage ceremonies considered appropriate solely for virgin girls. This situation is an example of how behavior often slips through the interstices of the customary and legal norms and gives rise to ambiguities.

Minimum Ceremony

The minimum ceremony for a virgin girl that generally is regarded as acceptable and that gives her the status of married woman consists of four elements. The daughter of Uma Maya, Dubal Singh's elder wife, was married in this way. The family of the young man who was interested in the girl made contact with Bom Bahadur, who was selected because he belonged to the group of men who had married girls from the young man's lineage. Bom Bahadur asked a woman Metalworker to go to ask Uma Maya whether she was willing to have her daughter marry this boy. She consented and Bom Bahadur came to her house and took her daughter to the boy's village. There, in the first of the four ritual elements—an element that only Vaishnavite Magar converts would omit—Bom

Bahadur sacrificed a chicken at the entrance to the lane into the boy's farmstead. For strength and well-being, and to keep evil spirits away, the bride first and then the groom stepped on the blood and entered the lane. The second element occurred at the door of the groom's house when first the father and his lineage brothers and then the mother gave the couple tikka of red-colored curd and rice. This was a token of their acceptance of the young couple, of their respect for them, and of their hopes for their future. When the couple had gone inside the house the groom gave the bride some bangles and a box of red powder for the part in her hair. Although she did not put the powder on then, but saved it to wear when she went out to some public place for the first time as a wife, putting on the powder is the third step. It symbolizes consummation of the marriage. The couple were fed by the groom's parents, and following the meal, began living together as man and wife, even though the final step in the marriage ceremony had not yet taken place. This occurred when they returned to Uma Maya carrying a gift of a little food. After receiving tikka from her and Dev Bahadur, her husband's brother, they entered her house and ate from her kitchen. The marriage now had been recognized and approved by both sets of parents, and by the natal lineages of each couple.

Beginning with this ceremony as a minimum, marriages of virgin girls can become more and more elaborate. The elaboration begins with the return to the girl's house to receive tikka from her parents and her father's lineage brothers. It is a matter of bringing more food and making the return more conspicuous. There may be negotiation on this point prior to the trip to the groom's house; if the girl has run away with the boy, it may take place afterwards. A very elaborate return for tikka from the bride's people would consist of one Tailor to beat a drum, and a virgin girl from the groom's lineage, plus a man married to one of the girls from his lineage. The man and girl carry curd, fried bread, beer, and distilled liquor made of rice.

Beyond this point, the elaboration includes the use of one or more Brahmans to conduct Vedic rites in Sanskrit. In its simplest form, the bride and groom come to the groom's house and at some time, either before or after they enter the groom's house with the minimum Magar rites, a Brahman performs simple Sanskritic rites involving at least the offering to fire. At its most elaborate, a marriage with Vedic rites involves a number of Brahmans, lengthy and complex rituals, many people and big feasts. Such a marriage is described as *ghurung-ghurung*—an onomatapoetic way of indicating the sound made by the many drums of the necessarily large Tailor band.

Remarriages

Although one tends to think of the new family beginning with the first marriage of a boy and girl, in fact almost all Banyan Hill families at the time of the research were founded on marriages between spouses who had been married more than once. In the hills it is not uncommon for wives, especially younger ones, to leave their husbands and marry another man. The first time a girl leaves her husband, she is called a *jari* girl or wife. If she leaves the second husband and marries a third, she is known as a *sari*. If she marries a fourth she may be spoken of (though not openly) as a *phundi,* a term of opprobrium connoting sexual looseness. The *jari* or *sari* wife is not regarded censoriously. If she suffers any disability, it is in the ritual sphere. At the time of a funeral, she is separated from girls married as virgins; she cannot make offerings of rice to the dead, and many persons would not eat black pulse or ground millet that she has cooked regardless of what rituals she may have observed in their preparation.

Very often the *jari* marriage depends upon the services of a go-between. When Padam Bahadur's first wife died leaving him with three sons, the father went to a Magar friend and the friend asked his wife to make enquiries in her natal village when she went there to visit. It was she who discovered Padam Bahadur's second wife and suggested to the girl's mother that she persuade her to run away from her absent soldier husband. Neither Padam nor his wife saw each other prior to her arrival.

In a *jari* or *sari* marriage, the essential ceremonies are the same as for a virgin girl. The same kind of affinal relative is asked to come and sacrifice the chicken, and parents of the new husband give the new wife tikka, though as a rule the lineage brothers of the groom's father are not expected to give tikka as they are expected to do in the case of a virgin girl. Second wives and widows are given bangles by their husbands but are not given red powder. The couple must go eventually to the girl's house to receive tikka from her parents, but they must not go before the new husband has paid compensation for his new wife. It is said that if they do, the parents, who have recognized the union by giving tikka, become responsible for paying the compensation. It is felt, too, that a wife should not meet her ex-husband before the compensation is paid.

Second marriages enter the sphere of politics. As soon as the husband who has been deserted discovers where his wife has gone, he goes to his headman. The headman arranges a meeting between himself and the headman of the man now living with the girl. When the meeting is held, numbers of men who are friends and relatives of each of the principals come to offer support and advice. Much depends upon the relative power of the two headmen. A strong headman will be able to obtain a larger *jari* payment for his client than a weak one; if he is on the other side, he will be able to get his client off with a small payment. Any assessment, though, is tailored realistically to what the new husband will be able to pay, and to some extent it reflects the character of the deserted husband. If he treated his wife well, even though she was not happy with him, he has some advantage in the bargaining. Legally, the payment for a *jari* wife is Rs 60, and Rs 30 for a *sari* wife. In every case for which I have records, these payments were exceeded, sometimes by a very large amount. It was commonly said, although I was unable to verify this to my satisfaction, that a headman's son in a neighboring village was able to collect Rs 2400. Between Rs 200 and Rs 500 was the usual payment in Banyan Hill. If a wife who has been married three times runs away, the husband cannot collect any compensation.

Abduction

To avoid the expense of marriage ceremonial parents of virgin girls sometimes arrange to have them abducted by a boy they have approved of as a husband. The eldest son of Kanchha Ba eventually married in this way, because neither his father nor his bride-to-be's parents wanted the expense of a more formal ceremony. Without the girl's knowledge, the two families agreed on a day when Kanchha Ba's son was to come and get her. Kanchha Ba's son asked an Ex-Slave man to come along to carry her, and he also asked some of his friends to help. The group went to the girl's village and lay in wait all one day in the nearby woods where the girl was expected to come to cut cattle fodder. When she did not appear, as a result of a mix-up in plan, the group went to her parents' house. Her parents called to her to come and meet some visitors, and when she appeared, the members of the group grabbed her and took her away forcibly. The girl bit her captors, cried out and struggled to free herself—acts that are expected, even though a girl may favor her abductor as a husband.

A girl who is abducted usually harbors some resentment against her parents. This is true, even though she understands that her parents would have had to go into debt to provide a more expensive type of marriage. But marriages by abduction generally are as successful as other types. The reason is that abduction usually occurs as a result of financial considerations and not because the parents think the girl would refuse to marry the groom they have selected.

Sheer captures, or captures that have not been arranged by the parents, are also a feature of hill life, although they are not very numerous. I would estimate that sheer capture and arranged abductions together account for only about 5 percent of all virgin marriages. Sheer capture is illegal, and a boy and his family who secure a girl in this way are liable to legal action if the parents of the girl wish to take this course. There are two factors that make this unlikely. One is community sentiment. It is customary for girls to be married before they have passed very far into their teens. In the case of girls whom the community regards as old enough to marry, there are fairly strong sentiments supporting the captor. It is felt that the parents should have expected this might happen, and if they wished to avoid it, they should have worked more diligently to secure a husband for their daughter. Support for the captor is especially strong when the parents permit a girl to join young people's singing groups and stay out late at night. The other factor that makes legal action less likely is the freedom a captured girl has to return to her own family or to run away with another man. It is a blow to the prestige of the captor and his family if a girl takes either of these two steps. The result is that young men and their relatives do not capture girls who come from a markedly different social stratum. They capture a girl who is likely to regard the match as suitable, for they realize that if the girl and her family cannot be persuaded to accept the match, she may run away or the family may take the matter to court.

Sometimes parents, or those who are acting as parents, do not support the objections of a captured girl. A soldier home on leave, who lived in a village near Banyan Hill, captured a girl who was singing one night with a group of friends, including some boys. The boys rescued her, but when she returned to her own house, her brother, who had been acting as her guardian following the death of her parents, refused to let her in. He approved the match, and in order to justify his refusal to take her back, he claimed she had lost her virginity to her captor and hence was "spoiled" for any other match. Faced with this attitude on the part of her brother, the girl went back to the soldier and married him.

Sometimes a young girl runs away with a boy without obtaining her parents' permission. This occurred twice with Om Bahadur's wife's daughter prior to the girl's elopement with Dhem Bahadur. She ran away with a boy from a nearby hamlet and stayed nine days. When the mother discovered where her daughter was, she went and dragged her home. In the eyes of the national law, the couple were legally married, because there was no bar and there was presumption of sexual intercourse. But as it worked out locally, the "husband" who had been deprived of his wife did not have any recourse. He went to see the headman of Banyan Hill and asked whether he would be able to collect compensation if his "wife" were to marry again. The headman told him that he would not be able to, because he and his "wife" had not obtained tikka from the girl's parents. This decision showed the local importance of securing parental blessing. Aside from customary and local legal considerations, there also were pressures to obtain this blessing because it was believed to be very inauspicious for either the girl or the boy to see parents until they had consented to give tikka—a consent that was only a problem on the girl's side and almost never was withheld for more than a few months if the girl insisted on leaving home.

Husband and Wife

The Banyan Hill family may be characterized in many ways as an amended and relaxed version of the traditional landowning Hindu family of the north Indian plains. In this type of family, the focus for authority and decision-making is the active elderly male. There are strong pressures to keep married sons in the family. Patterns of interpersonal behavior help to maintain this unity and make it more feasible. Sons show much deference to fathers and avoid them when they are not alone. Younger brothers behave in a similar fashion toward elder brothers, the men who one day may assume the role of family head. Young married couples avoid one another during the day and leave the training and disciplining of their children to the elders. By these rules, the tendency for each nuclear family to become a domain unto itself and thus disrupt the larger extended family is played down and weakened. Just as sons are expected to be obedient to the father and to show him much deference, wives are expected to defer to husbands, and, in the domestic sphere, to the husband's mother. On the plains of India such families often are like citadels and have an embattled quality. There are lines of cooperation with other families, but to a great degree each stands against the others. Authority, discipline, deference, self-abnegation, subordination of women, are important values in such a social system.

In the Banyan Hill type of family, the father also is the focal figure of authority, and in many other ways the patterning slopes in the direction of the traditional Hindu family. But while the pattern is frequently realized in India, it often, in many dimensions, is only hinted at in Banyan Hill or carried only a little way toward full expression. A basic reason for the difference would seem to be lack of emphasis upon the strong, often almost militantly strong, extended family. This, in turn, may bear a close relationship both to the fact that in the hills farms are smaller and to the fact that pressures on the land have not reached the same critical point as on the plains. Values no doubt also play a part. The extreme competitiveness and sensitivity to slight status differences characteristic of much village life in the plains is softened in the hills. It is part of this general difference that one does not find either as widespread or as intense an emphasis upon political jockeying. In the hills, more families can be politically neutral or relatively indifferent. Taken all together, these factors provide a context in which the more full-blown development of patterns found in the plains-type Indian patriarchal, extended family, become less necessary.

Perhaps the major difference between the two types of family is the emphasis that the Magars place upon the husband and wife. Soon after sons marry, they generally set up their own establishments, and among the Banyan Hill Magars there were no instances of brother living with brother. In such families, there is no bar to a strong erotic and affectionate tie between husband and wife, and when such a tie does not exist, there is opportunity to terminate the marriage.

The scenes that follow convey the essence of the husband-wife relationship in Banyan Hill. Maila Ba is plowing and his youngest wife walks behind dropping seeds into the furrow; he is churning on his porch while his eldest wife stands just behind him with a metal pan, waiting for him to drop the ropes he has been pulling back and forth and then scoop the white butter from the top of the churn and give it to her for heating. The Admara headman is sitting on the floor in the upper storey of his *dhansar*. He is sharing the hukka with his wife who sits just across from him, and they are talking quietly together. The Havildar Major is squatting in his kitchen-eating room. He is facing the wall, at the place where the Household Godling is worshipped, and he holds a chicken in his hands. His wife stands just to one side and behind. She will hand him the sickle when it is time to sacrifice the cock and a pan to catch the blood. During the heat of noon, Bir Bahadur, his wife, and his son are sleeping side by side on rice-straw mats inside his open-sided storage shed. These are scenes of a life shared in a great many spheres of activity, with a minimum of avoidance. The basic tone is one of easy companionship.

Of course, this is not the whole picture; it is only the middle and most common range of behavior and feeling. To make it complete, one must point to the existence of a patriarchal bias and then explain how it is countered by patterns that bring power and independence to the wife.

Patriarchal Bias vs. Independence of Women

The patriarchal bias arises because Magar society emphasizes the male line. It is from his father that a boy receives his lineage affiliation. As a member of this group, a boy secures property rights not shared with his sister. If unmarried, a girl can claim a share of her father's farmstead, but she cannot claim a share of the property of a member of her father's lineage should one of them die heirless. When it comes time for him to marry, the boy brings his wife from her home to his home or neighborhood. He is on familiar ground; she is the newcomer and must make the greater adjustment. The man has more freedom of movement than the wife. Though the wife often accompanies the husband on long trading trips or trips to holy places, he can if he wishes go alone. The wife or the unmarried girl cannot. There are many situations in which the wife is expected to show deference to the husband. In the morning she is expected to get up first and she begins the day by filling a small jug of water, going to her husband's mat, and pouring a little water over his big toe. She catches some in her cupped palm, and in a gesture of respect that implies he is god-like, touches some to her lips. She should never eat before her husband has eaten; if he is late in returning home, she should feed the children, but should herself refrain from eating until he comes. On the trail, the husband walks first and the wife follows behind. If something is to be carried that is not too heavy, such as food, extra clothing, or a child, the woman carries it. She even carries her husband's coat if he gets warm and takes it off.

In the most important festival of the year, Dasain, the focal figures are males—the father, the brother, and the eldest male in the lineage. And to some extent, deference for the husband is reinforced by the rule that a younger person defers to an older, because a husband generally is older than a wife.

In the more general cultural sphere, the pervasive influence of Hinduism in this section of the hills supports the husband as one to whom the wife should defer. The story of the *Ramayana* is well-known, with its picture of Sita, the sweetly loyal and deferential wife. Although in the Hindu religious rite of Satya Narayan, both husband and wife participate together, in another very important Hindu ceremony, the offering of rice balls to the ancestors, it is the husband alone who performs. Hinduism also emphasizes the male by giving the son a crucially important role to play in the funeral rites.

Among the high castes of northern India, emphasis upon the patriarchal theme is found with comparatively little to counterbalance it. In this section of Nepal, especially among tribes such as the Magars, there are many things that act with contrary effect. The result is a relationship between husband and wife whose over-all coloring is quite different.

Although the new wife may move into the house of her parents-in-law and live there for a short time, it is understood that the new couple soon will establish a separate home of their own. Thus even when girls are living in their husbands' homes, there is not a highly authoritarian and submissive relationship between mothers-in-law and daughters-in-law. An indication of the relaxed relation between mother-in-law and daughter-in-law, could be seen at Bom Bahadur's. One day the daughter-in-law, who was sitting on the verandah, was tickling her dozing mother-in-law's feet with a straw.

The daughter-in-law is very respectful in the presence of the father-in-law. But her deferential attitude is combined with a freedom to speak. The Subedar's son was in the army and the son's wife was living with her father-in-law. Before the son went back to the army following his leave, during which he got married, he obtained his father's permission to have a small house of his own, using materials from one of his father's sheds. Nothing was done for some time following his departure. Finally the daughter-in-law took the initiative and approached her husband's father. She indicated respect by addressing him in a whiny, singsong "woman's" voice and by keeping her eyes averted from his and her shawl before her mouth. But she did speak out and was not regarded as willful. In addition, she also went to Kanchha Ba and, showing the same kind of respectful behavior combined with determination, reminded him that he had promised to do the heavy work in converting the shed into a new house.

An important support for a wife is a gift (*pewa*) that is given to her by her parents when she marries. Husbands have no right to this kind of property; it belongs solely to the wife to do with as she pleases. For many girls *pewa* consisted of livestock such as goats, cows, or buffaloes. Chickens also are a common gift. By breeding the animals, women were able to increase their stock; when they needed small amounts of cash for spending on trinkets at a bazaar, they could perhaps sell some of them. *Pewa* sometimes also consisted of land, and a wealthy father might give his daughter a plot of paddy. Rice land provided a steady, generous, and independent source of income for a married daughter; some used such income to make loans. Although *pewa* was closely associated with marriage, since it was most often given at that time, it could also be given throughout the course of a daughter's life. Frequently, a daughter would come back from a visit to her father and mother or a brother with a chicken or two; if she belonged to one of the wealthier families and had gone home for a funeral, she might return with a calf or a cow. It was significant, too, that few natal homes of wives were more than five miles distant. Wives went home frequently, and the tie was continually strengthened by festival visiting and exchange of gifts.

Further support lay in the fact that at marriage a woman acquired a share in her husband's property. Initially, when there were no children, she had a right to use and secure income from half his property, provided she did not remarry. This right persisted even if she did not live with her husband. Only marriage dissolved her lien. At birth, each child also acquired a share so that shares in the father's and husband's property kept diminishing in size as the family grew. But whatever the wife's share was, it remained hers until death, when it reverted to her husband's estate. This right was very significant, because it meant that no matter what the emotional content of her marriage, and no matter whether the husband took other wives, she still could look to her husband's farm for some support.

If a wife was not happy with her husband, two paths were open to her. She could return to her natal home, or she could run away with another man. Very often the first step was a precursor of the second. As a rule, children remained with the father, since even the girls had a right to a share in their father's land up until the time of their marriage. The existence of easy separation and divorce encouraged husbands to treat wives well, if they wished to keep them. One did not hear of wife beating in Banyan Hill, nor of wives committing suicide.

Surely one of the basic reasons for a woman's high status was the essential and many-faceted part she played in forwarding the domestic economy. Banyan Hill wives were too poised and good-natured to give the impression of being drudges, but they did work very hard. After plowing they went about in the fields swinging a mattock to break up the clods. They weeded and planted, carried wood, water, and manure. They cared for the farm animals and did the milking. Older women usually did not climb the highest trees for fodder, but they did gather leaves from bushes, cut grass, carry wood, plant paddy, and weed every crop. In the early morning, sometimes long before dawn, one heard them operating the hulling beams and winnowing the chaff. They spent many hours at the stone grinding mills and many more hours squatting by the fireplaces cooking. They also spent much of every day in the courtyard processing food.

These labors constantly reinforced a sense of economic interdependence, a sense that was given additional strength by the lack of any very rigid division of labor according to the sex of individuals. There are some tasks such as plowing that are strictly reserved for men. But there are many other tasks that can be done by either men or women and often are done by men and women together. Husbands and wives join groups that go fishing together. Women mostly work the foot-operated rice huller, but men frequently are seen doing it while the wife sits at the hole dropping in more rice and taking out the chaff. Men without daughters cook when their wives are menstruating, and a man has to learn tasks normally reserved for the woman because he travels. When a group of men go on a trek to a border town for trading, they carry their food and do their own cooking. Once on a trek our porters purchased some gritty rice that had to be winnowed before it could be cooked. For days on the trail one of the men, by group decision the expert, winnowed the dirt from the rice and did it very well. But when we stopped to cook one noon by a spring where many Magar women were washing their clothes and hair, he went up to one of the older women and said, "Elder sister, would you winnow this dirty rice for me? I do not know how to do it." She willingly consented, though with no better results than he had been achieving.

All these factors—the close connection with the natal home, right to *pewa* and property, right to remarry or to leave, a vital role in the subsistence pattern, plus the lack of a rigid division of labor—help give the wife high status and assurance and play a large part in mitigating the culture's patriarchal bias.

There are other factors that contribute to the kind of husband-wife relationship found in Banyan Hill, and here one thinks not so much of its economic and legal facets as of its affectionate, erotic side. Because of the cooperative work groups and the singing groups, young people who are old enough to marry have an opportunity for close association. This means that even though first marriages generally are arranged, young people who marry may know and even prefer one another. It also means that if they do not achieve a satisfactory relationship, each has known other persons of the opposite sex, often with some intimacy, and can leave the marriage with some confidence that they can find a more satisfactory substitute. Also, it is quite generally true that first marriages are not apt to be the marriages that are longest lasting or produce the most children. Very often first marriages end in divorce and not infrequently the first wife dies usually as a result of complications connected with childbirth. Established marriages generally are second or third marriages, and they are alliances that both parties have entered into with some experience.

The majority of Banyan Hill marriages are monogamous, and most marriages rest upon mutual fidelity. Adultery of course does occur, and the consequences may be different for a husband than for a wife. The wife who commits adultery, or wishes to, will run away from her husband. The marriage cannot continue. Husbands have a wider range of alternatives. A husband—this is especially true of young ones—may continue to attend songfests and may have an occasional casual affair. Affairs of any kind are almost impossible to hide, so the wife generally finds out. The marriage usually will not break up unless the wife feels neglected or abused, or unless the husband neglects his responsibilities to the farm. The marriage also is more likely to persist if the husband has a large estate in which the wife can expect to share.

A husband who has means also may take a second wife. The headman's eldest son's first marriage was to a high status girl and was largely a matter of establishing an alliance between the two families. His second marriage was established because he desired the enhanced status that two wives would give him; he also wanted many children and found the second girl sexually attractive. There is no doubt that the size of his estate was important in keeping his first wife with him when he married again, for she did feel anxiety as a result of the addition to the household. This was seen when she visited the shaman to obtain help in retaining her husband's attention and to make sure she would become pregnant and bear a son.

Another polygynous household, Dubal Singh's, was established when his first wife had only daughters. His desire for sons was so strong that he took another wife despite the fact that he was a very poor man and was finding it difficult enough to support one wife. An irony of the situation was that partly as a result of impoverishment due to his second marriage, which did not produce a son either, he had to go to India to work. Soon after he left, his first wife gave birth to a boy.

As we have seen, Maila Ba's was a polygynous household established for economic reasons. In his household the eldest wife did the cooking and looked after the daughter of the absent third wife. She also cared for the barnyard animals, including the buffaloes. The young wife went much more often to the fields and worked there. This division was not rigid, however, because the eldest wife also did fieldwork when help was needed. She assisted when there was manure to be carried, she broke up clods and harvested. Both wives worked together at hulling rice and at grinding. But only the eldest wife participated with Maila Ba when he was honoring the Household Godling. On a festival occasion such as Dasain, Maila Ba paid visits to the natal homes of both wives, remaining at each for a day. Maila Ba's bed was on the porch, and unless it was very cold he slept there. The eldest wife slept in the main room of the house or in one of the two *dhansars*. The youngest wife had a room of her own at the end of the verandah. The ménage was a successful one, with a very smooth and tension-free intermeshing of the lives and tasks of the three adults. The youngest wife was very shy and retiring; the eldest, who had passed her childbearing years, did not feel threatened by her. Also, Maila Ba was discreet in his attentions to the young wife and seldom spoke to her in the presence of his eldest wife. When he did speak to her at any length, it usually was when they were working together side-by-side at a task such as harvesting wheat straw.

Lest this picture of husband and wife relations seem unrealistically free of tension and suppressed aggression, it would be well to recall a scene that takes place in the groom's village. On the evening when all the adult men have left to accompany the groom to the bride's village as members of his wedding procession, the married women gather at the groom's house. Some of them are dressed up in their husbands' old army uniforms, and one or two of them have tied large phalli to themselves. With loud merriment, the group sing songs that are explicitly erotic. While some of the women try to dance, those with phalli chase them and pretend to force them to have sexual intercourse. The women who take the part of the men are the focal figures, and their rendition of the sexually aroused male is satirical and immensely amusing to the group.

5

Family: Family Cycle

Early Childhood

A RESULT of the relation between most husbands and wives is that children are born into homes where tensions between adults are minimal. They also are born into homes where children are much desired and liked. It is true that a boy baby is more wanted than a girl. Pregnant mothers and mothers hoping to conceive visit the shaman for spells or go to local shrines to pray that they bear a son. When a first son is born, wealthier families have a feast and invite relatives and neighbors on the sixth day following the birth. Yet despite this preference, daughters also are highly regarded and are treated with much affection. In its extreme form, a male cultural bias can lead to female infanticide or, when less extreme, to involuntary female infanticide through neglect. In Banyan Hill, there was no evidence of either type of death. Unmarried girls of the family and lineage have high ritual value. Gifts given to them are like gifts to goddesses and are a way of obtaining religious merit. This also is true in India, but in the hills the ritual value of daughters is an enhancement of their greater economic value. Daughters are a more important source of labor than on the plains, since the pool of landless laborers in the hills is smaller. It is hard to imagine some Magar farms operating if daughters were not permitted to do many kinds of hard farm labor.

The naming ceremony, which always is performed by a Brahman, marks the beginning of a child's life as a unique, named individual. It also permits the mother to become active again and removes the pollution of birth from her household and from the members of her husband's lineage. The state of pollution (removed by the naming ceremony) begins three months before the child's birth. At this time, and until the time of the birth, the mother can cook meals for the family; she must refrain from active participation in religious ceremonials. It would be possible, for example, to hold a Satya Narayan ceremony at the house; instead of participating directly with her husband in the worship as she normally would, she now has to stand aside.

The birth takes place in the small room off the main room, the furthest from the entrance door and the darkest in the house. Occasionally, a woman from the community with a reputation for midwifery will be called, especially when the birth is difficult. Usually a woman asks a neighbor to help or her own daughter, if the girl is eight years old or more. For ten days the mother and baby remain inside the house out of the sunlight, for the sight of mother and child in a state of pollution is offensive to this holy luminary. They also remain apart from the other members of the family. During this period, a daughter, husband, or perhaps the mother's sister does the cooking; the new mother must not touch the water containers or any of the cooking utensils.

When the Brahman comes to perform the naming ceremony on the eleventh day following the birth, he first purifies the house by sprinkling a little cow urine inside and outside, and then he gives a little to each family member so that they can purify themselves by touching it to their lips. Following a puja, which he conducts on the verandah, the Brahman writes three names on three leaves from a pipal tree. The first name is drawn from his astrological tables and is reckoned according to the date and times of the birth. The second name refers to the season of the birth and the third to the day. Thus, a girl who was born on April 12, 1961 was named Sheku, since the astrological tables said her name should begin with *She*. This name will be used if she marries according to Hindu rites conducted by a Brahman or when she participates under the guidance of a Brahman in a ceremony such as the Satya Narayan puja. The spring months of Chaitre (March–April) and Baisakh (April–May) are called *basant,* so her second name —the one the family said they would use—was Basanta. Since she was born on Wednesday (*Budhabar*) her third name was Budha. This name was the least important, and it would not be used for anything except to remind the family of the day she was born.

While a member of the family holds the baby, the Brahman rolls up the leaves one at a time to form a tube, then he blows the respective names into the baby's ear along with a spell in Sanskrit. As a final act in the ceremony, he and the father give tikka to unmarried daughters in the baby's family and to unmarried daughters of the father's lineage members who may be present. The father also bows down and touches his head to the feet of these girls, gives each a few pice, and puts some flowers in their hair.

Parents hope for as many children as possible. Their usefulness as labor and as supports in old age are more important than their cost as additional mouths to feed and bodies to clothe. Since there is no taboo on sexual relations once the mother has recovered from the birth, children can follow each other in almost yearly succession. They grow up in the center of the day-to-day life of the household. The nursing baby sleeps with the mother on a straw mat. During the day it spends many hours in a coarsely woven hammock slung between posts of the verandah. The sides are high enough so that the child cannot possibly fall out. When it wakes and is fretful, the mother, or whoever is nearby, gives the hammock a push. If rocking does not still it, it will be nursed and fondled. On trips away from the house, the mother carries the baby in a cloth sling across her back. When she goes to the spring, or for some other reason must carry a basket on her back, she places the baby in the basket and it rides on a folded blanket on top of the load.

Toilet training is gradual and is done without fuss. Weaning, too, is nontraumatic. When a boy is about six months old, and a girl about five, an astrologer is called to determine a suitable day for giving the baby its first taste of rice. A wealthy family may invite relatives and neighbors for a feast on this day, though generally the ceremony is limited to members of the household. The feeding consists only of touching rice to the child's mouth. An unmarried girl, preferably a real or lineage sister, does this first; then it is done by each member of the family in turn. Until this ceremony, the baby has worn clothing made of previously used cloth. Now for the first time the parents give it a garment—usually a shirt—made from new cloth. The first rice feeding ceremony does not constitute weaning, but from now on the child will be given solid food if it will eat it. A pregnant mother will try to hurry the weaning; otherwise a child is given the breast whenever it demands, even until it is three or four years old. During the process of weaning, mother, father, and children all do what they can to distract the child and get it to eat solid food.

A toddler rides about on the parent's hip or on an older brother's or sister's. When the father goes to graze his goats or cows, he often takes the child with him, especially a boy. Parents also take small children with them when they go on pilgrimages to holy places. But a young child spends much of its time crawling about in the courtyard and the house. Inside the house, the worst hazard is the open firepit; outside, a fall from the verandah, or very rarely, an encounter with a centipede. Children of this age get very dirty. Adults wash themselves often in the cold water of the springs. But except for hands and face, washing is not forced on children because they do not like it. As a result, many children have sores on their legs which do not heal until they do wash more frequently.

When a girl is about three years old, her parents give her a new shirt. The astrologer is not consulted, but the gift is made on a day of the week, such as Tuesday, which is regarded as more auspicious than others. In the minds of the parents, this rite of passage for the girl corresponds to the more elaborate hair cutting ceremony for the boy, which takes place when he is about five years old.

The hair cutting ceremony of Indra Jit, the son of Saila Ba, took place when he was four and a half. As was customary, a lineage uncle was in charge. In Indra Jit's case, this was the Havildar Major; the ceremony took place in the Havildar Major's cow shed. The boy did not want to go to the ceremony, and his mother had to carry him. Normally his father would have taken him, but he had to be away from home that day. Indra Jit wore a new cotton shawl. His uncle placed him next to a cow stanchion on a low wooden stool. After placing the cow's tether rope around the boy's neck, thus associating him with that holy animal, he turned him so that the boy was facing east. During the cutting when he occasionally turned away from this direction, the Havildar Major would gently move him back again, for east is felt to be the most auspicious of all directions.

After knotting the lock at the crown of the head, which a Hindu never cuts, the Havildar clipped the boy's hair with a pair of scissors. Whenever the boy cried, his uncle offered him a piece of rock sugar candy that he had brought on a leaf plate. The Havildar collected the shorn locks in another leaf plate and said they would be placed in the rafters of his own house and kept there forever. The boy's older sister also was present and she kept trying to feed him a banana and some fried bread that she had brought. Beside her there were six little children, both boys and girls, standing about watching. All were from the boy's own family or from the Havildar's or the Headman's.

When all the hair except the Hindu lock had been cut off, the Havildar, to stimulate vigorous new growth, rubbed some mustard oil into the boy's scalp and put a new shirt on him to symbolize his new status. The garment had been completed on a sewing machine by a Tailor woman who had been called to Saila Ba's house just the day before. She also had made two caps, one to be given to the boy by the father, the other by the Havildar. The Havildar put both of them on Indra Jit's head, one on top of the other. As a further sign of his hopes for the boy, and to honor him and give him a memento of the ceremony, he gave him tikka. With some red paste that had been mixed in a leaf plate, he made a dot with one finger on the boy's forehead and then, as an avuncular joke, on the tip of his nose. Then, as a further sign of hope and respect, he tucked two small yellow flowers up under his new caps. In concluding the ceremony, the Havildar took the cow tether from Indra Jit's neck and led him over to where the other children were standing. There he gave him five pice and told him he should honor his sister and give the pice to her. Indra Jit knelt down and touched his forehead to his youngest sister's feet and gave her the money. In turn, helped by his uncle, he made the same respectful gesture and gave the same gift to each of the remaining unmarried girls of his lineage who were present: his own elder sister, his grandfather's daughter, his grandfather's son's daughter, and the Havildar's daughter. When he had honored these girls, the Havildar gave him a leaf plate full of curds and led him home. Curds are auspicious, and Indra Jit's family would share them as a commemorative food.

Later Childhood

From the age of about eight the child, whether boy or girl, gradually is asked to assist with household and farm tasks. The daughter is given a basket and tumpline and begins to fill and carry small jugs of water from the spring. Maila Ba's daughter, who was eleven, was expected to go with her eldest stepmother to the spring early each morning and help her carry back the day's supply of water. The stepmother's attempts to wake the girl invariably were greeted with whining complaints, and these were reiterated whenever she was urged to get up and get her basket, tumpline, and waterpot. Frequently she got under way only when the father came and interceded with a firm request. The children at the Headman's household next door did not whine nearly as much when they were asked to do things, but they were not cowed either. The Headman was the first up in the morning; on his way to the nearby woods to the latrine he would call out, "Get up! Get up!" as he passed the verandah where the children were sleeping. But on his return, it was seldom that he did not have to stop and call a few more times, and even prod, to get the children on their feet. The general atmosphere, even in this household, which perhaps was the strictest of all, was relaxed. Neither here nor in any home during the course of our stay in Banyan Hill did we see an instance of corporal punishment, nor even of a lengthy and harsh berating. Children's lack of fear of parents, especially the mother, was evident during interviews, which were continually being interrupted by youngsters, who, despite urgings and orders to go away for a bit, would keep on teasing for food. Almost always the mothers, and sometimes a father, eventually would get up and get some food. On trips with their parents, the children always teased for sweets when passing through trailside bazaars, and most parents would manage to provide them with something.

Younger children and children who have begun to work spend much of their time in neighborhood playgroups. Sometimes one of the children will make off with some grain from the household storage bin. He will collect his friends and they will go off into the woods, where they will build a small fire to parch the grain and have a clandestine picnic. Occasionally, children can also persuade their parents to let them have a few pice, so that they can walk to the Deorali bazaar and purchase a little rock sugar candy or some plain sugar if that is not available.

Tasks are divided among the children following the same pattern as among adults. Girls learn to cook, weave, and carry manure. Boys learn to butcher livestock, make sacrifices to the godlings, make baskets, nets, and ropes, put on thatch, and plow. Both boys and girls learn to spin, operate the oil mill, rice huller, and grindstone, carry water and milk, make rice straw mats, get fodder, and catch fish. When children are about twelve, they can do almost all adult tasks and can be genuine assets to the household. Sometimes a child is so valuable to the family economy that he has to forego schooling, as was the case with the Havildar Major's eldest son.

Children are taught to show respect for their parents. Whenever a boy has been away for any length of time and returns home, he greets his mother and father by placing his forehead on their feet. A girl's gesture is less deferential, since she has a higher ritual status than her brother. When a daughter greets her parents after being away, she only covers her head, bows forward from the waist, and extends her right arm, holding her left hand under the elbow. For the most part, though, relations between parents and older children are quite informal. Parents and children sit together on the porch of the house, and if a boy or girl is sitting and the father comes into the yard or up to the porch, they do not get up. The son does not avoid sitting near the father. When there is a formal gathering of adult men, he may sit on the same resting place, but to one side. Children smoke in their parents' presence. Girl children are excluded from the part of a religious ceremony involving live sacrifice, but afterwards, when the animal is being cooked, they come and join their father and brothers. There is sufficient restraint between fathers and sons so that they do not argue when they disagree. When a boy in his late teens wishes to enlist in the army despite his parents' objections, the arguments are most likely to occur between the mother and son. The boy may express his opinion once or twice to the father but does not press it. The usual way for breaking such a deadlock is for the son to join a friend or a group from a number of nearby villages and run away.

A girl's first menstruation is not marked ceremoniously, but she is subject to a number of restrictions for a fifteen-day period. At the onset, she must segregate herself from her father and brothers and must remain out of the sunlight. She must also stay away from the kitchen and refrain from touching anyone's food or water. After the first five days of this segregation, which for convenience often is passed in the home of a widow friend, the girl can come out into the sunlight, although for two more days she must not do any work in the fields. When the seventh day has passed, she can do fieldwork but still cannot cook, handle the family's cooking utensils or water pots, or touch men. She usually comes back to her own house after the fifth day, but her food is prepared by others and she eats separately. On the fifthteenth day, she goes to a spring, washes herself and her clothing, and puts on clean clothes. Back at home she is given water that has been touched by gold. By wetting her head with it three times and drinking some of it three times, she attains complete freedom from pollution.

Sibling Relations

Terminologically, a distinction is made among all brothers. In a household containing six brothers, the boys would be addressed respectively from oldest to youngest as *jetha, maila, saile, kaila, raila,* and *kanchha.* In ritual contexts, this order has some importance. At Dasain, for example, the eldest would be the first to receive tikka from the father and the others would receive it in order of birth. In a headman's family, it is the eldest son who is expected to inherit, if he is competent. Thus, there is some stress on differences in age, and these differences are given terminological emphasis. But the stress is countered somewhat by the rule that all sons inherit equally and by the generally egalitarian nature of the lineage. In day-to-day social relations, brothers close to one another in age participate almost as equals. They go to songfests together, eat and drink communally-purchased meals with their mutual friends, and accompany one another to distant *melas.* There is no shyness and avoidance, and I never saw an elder brother pull rank on a younger. There is a bit more seeming formality, perhaps, between brothers who are further apart in age. But this is more a result of having different friends and of moving in different social spheres than anything inherent in the relationship. In tone and pattern, the relationships between sisters closely resemble those between brothers.

Brothers and sisters play together during childhood, and the relation remains close throughout life. Once a year, during Dasain, the close relationship between a brother and his married sister is given ritual expression; from time to time a brother may stop at his sister's house informally to see how she is. He always greets her by placing his forehead on her feet. When in trouble, a sister always feels she can turn to a brother. A brother rather than the father is more apt to come to her house to assist her, for example, in harvesting; he can eat there, whereas the father is not supposed to take any food at his daughter's home or even in her village. Following the death of the father, the brother becomes a father surrogate and will do all he can to help a needy sister. The headman of Banyan Hill exemplifies approved brotherly behavior, for he helped provide land and a house for both his youngest and his eldest sisters.

Funeral

In Banyan Hill, one may pass through the ceremonies that mark off the middle portions of one's life without the assistance of a Brahman. That is, one may pass from childhood into preadulthood (through the hair cutting ceremony) or into adulthood (through the marriage ceremony) all without hearing Sanskrit or participating in Vedic rituals. But the initial naming ceremony and the final funeral ceremony both require Brahmanical assistance. As with marriages, there is much variety in the funeral rites, which differ according to the age, sex, and wealth of the deceased. In minimum rites for an adult male, the dying man is purified by being given water to drink that has been touched with gold. After death, his son and other members of his lineage carry the body to the river, where it usually is released in the water. Some bodies are buried; only a few are cremated because it requires too many people to carry the wood, and the necessary butter and vegetable oil are so expensive. On returning from the river, the sons and their wives segregate themselves and observe many restrictions for thirteen days. On the thirteenth day, a Brahman is called and with cow urine and offerings to fire, he removes pollution from all members of the dead man's lineage and family. In a final ceremony, the Brahman is given gifts, for gifts given to a Brahman will be translated to the other world for use by the deceased. Even poor families frequently will spend large sums for gifts to Brahmans at this time.

The essential persons in a funeral are lineage members to carry the body, a real son or a lineage son to segregate himself during the period between the death and removal of pollution, a Brahman to restore a state of purity and to help the deceased in his journey to the other world, and married daughters plus their husbands. The daughters bring food for funeral guests; their husbands, who may also have helped carry the body to the river, erect pens of bamboo matting for sons and daughters-in-law of the deceased who are segregating themselves. In addition, they make an offering to the ancestral spirits in the kitchen-room, pray that they remain in the other world and not trouble the deceased's family, clean the house at the end of the period of pollution, take down and burn the segregation pens, and sacrifice a chicken so that each member of the deceased's household can dip his finger in the blood as further protection from the evil that causes death and is associated with it.

A Brahman may or may not be called at other times during the period when a family faces death. When older people of means are dying, a Brahman usually is called so they can make him a gift of a cow. It is believed that they will be able to hang onto the tail of this cow when there are difficult rivers to ford in the other world. Brahmans are also sometimes called at various times during the period of pollution following death.

Widowed mothers are supported by their sons, although some sons are more conscientious about this than others. Lakshmi Devi's older sons were totally responsible for her support, and they worked diligently for her and the younger children. The son of Tara Maya, youngest sister of the Headman, was much more lax about doing farm work. In part, no doubt, this was because he knew his mother could hire labor to do the tasks he neglected to do. She frequently chided him good-naturedly for his laziness but without much effect, and he continued making plans to follow his elder brother into the army. He felt free to take this course because she was not destitute and also because she could depend upon her brother for assistance. Dev Bahadur and Padam Bahadur both were caring for widowed mothers, and Bom Bahadur and Teg Bahadur both were responsible for widowed mothers-in-law.

Ancestor Spirits

A person who has died does not cease being a member of the family. He continues to be aware of his descendants and can affect them. His descendants, in turn, continue to be aware of him and realize that what they do controls, at least partially, the way he treats them. There are two kinds of deceased ancestor. One, called *bai,* is a godling who wanders about on earth and likes sacrificial blood. The other, called *pitri,* is in heaven and does not like sacrificial blood.

There are a number of reasons why a deceased family member becomes a *bai. Bai* include those who did not perform religiously-sanctioned good deeds during the course of their lives; those whose dead bodies were touched by some polluting animal, such as a dog, chicken, or crow; those who were witches; and men who were shamans. Finally, even persons who in the ordinary course would not become *bai,* may be stopped on their way to heaven by a witch or a shaman who have become *bai* and made to return to earth and begin troubling their family. The existence of *bai* points to concern about contributing to community welfare, anxiety about pollution and correct ritual procedure, and to the ambiguous feelings with which a shaman and his powers for good or evil are regarded. With the exception of their soldier ancestors, families regard forebears as *bai* who died violent and unexpected deaths. So far as could be ascertained, these *bai* are the only ones believed to affect a wider range of persons than their descendants. They are feared and placated by others as *mari.*

Except for *bai* who also are *mari,* these godlings never trouble people who are not their descendants. When considering his ancestors, a man may be sure that there were *bai* in many ascending generations. But it is believed generally that the *bai* that matter are those who begin with the grandfather and grandmother on his father's side, followed by all their male descendants and their wives. Even a son or grandson theoretically, although never so far as could be ascertained in actuality, could become a *bai.* With regard to *bai* who fall outside this range, Dev Bahadur said he told the older ones he was finding it impossible to honor them any more, and bid them goodbye. Some families are not at all troubled by *bai,* and Padam Bahadur's was one. He attributed this to the fact that his immediate ancestors gave cows to Brahmans before they died.

Bai are worshipped regularly once a year, and most families do puja for their *bai* on the spring full-moon day. Shrines for *bai* generally are found in open fields near large stones. A separate puja is done for each *bai.*

There is a way of exorcising *bai* permanently, and this was done by the Banyan Hill headman. A man far enough back in the line so that he was a common ancestor for all members of the Sinjali Thapa lineage in Banyan Hill had been a shaman. As a very old man, even while he was alive, he was suspected of being a witch and of using spells for evil purposes. When he died he became a *bai* and was very troublesome for the lineage as a whole. On a pilgrimage to holy places in India, the Headman stopped at Banares and did a ceremony for exorcising all *bai* in his lineage but in particular for the spirit of the troublesome shaman. As a result, none of the Headman's brothers do *bai* pujas nor does the collateral line closest to his, which includes Dirgha Singh and the Havildar Major. The members of his lineage from Darkang, however, have not accepted the reputed efficacy of the ceremony and continue to do pujas to their *bai,* although they do exclude the spirit of the shaman and consider him at least to have been rendered harmless.

When *bai* become troublesome despite annual pujas to them, the shaman, or whoever determines why they are unhappy, generally finds that they want a larger share of their descendants' estate. Commonly, the desired additional share is a chicken—a cock for a male and a hen for a female.

The *bai* are only capable of doing evil or refraining. *Pitri* can do both good or evil, although they generally are regarded as benevolent. There are two ways of worshipping *pitri,* one followed by those who are guided by Brahmans and the other by those who are not. For commemorating his ancestors, Maila Ba and a Brahman always performed the very ancient Hindu ceremony of *sraddha.* For this purpose, Maila Ba called the family Brahman to his house three times a year—on the anniversary of the deaths of his father and mother and once again during a portion of a month in the fall (September–October, 1961) that corresponded by calculations based on the Hindu calendar, to the day in this period that matched the actual day of his father's death. This period is called *pitri aunsi.*

The Headman did not join Maila Ba or his other brothers in these commemorations because he had made offerings to his forebears at the shrine of Badrinath in the Indian Himalayas. He had been taught that once this had been done it was not necessary to make yearly offerings.

When Maila Ba made his offering on the anniversary of his mother's death, he made an appointment with his family Brahman. He then asked Teg Bahadur, an affinal relative, to come and shave his head. He fasted before the ceremony, which took place on his porch in the early morning. After the Brahman had conducted a sanctifying puja, Maila Ba made the food offering, which consisted of balls of cooked rice mixed with cow's milk, curd, butter, honey, boiled sugar cane, barley, and sesame. Barefoot and wearing only a white cotton skirt, he put the rice balls on a leaf plate and carried them to a spring where he let them wash away. Any spring is regarded as holy and therefore a fit place in which to leave such an oblation.

Most men in Banyan Hill followed a pattern of *pitri* worship that brought them to a spring, but they made the puja on different days and in a different way. The time of the worship was not governed by the death anniversaries of their mother and father. It always took place on the first day of the month of Magh (January–February) and on the last day of the special period in the fall when those who followed the Brahman pattern made their third observance (*pitri aunsi*).

When Bom Bahadur made his Magh offering, he went to the spring near his house, bathed and put on a clean loincloth. After washing the surface of a flat stone, he spread banana leaves and on these placed a row of nine plates made of leaves from the jhankri bush. As an offering to his ancestors, he filled the plates with a mixture of hulled rice, black pulse, tumeric, barley, and sesame. A tenth plate was filled and set aside for the ancestors' porter. The puja at the spring was complete when he added a bit of ginger to each plate, filled a leaf plate with water, lighted a mustard oil lamp, and made incense of butter and sage leaves. The final act was giving some money and a tikka made of colored rice to his unmarried daughters. His offering made in the fall on *pitri aunsi* was the same, except that following the custom, no tumeric and black pulse were included.

When offerings to the *pitri* are made by the Brahman, he specifies which maternal and paternal ancestors are being included. When the Magar men make the offering themselves, they mention the ancestors when they make incense, but they do not specify any particular ones. Some insight into the general attitude toward these supernatural extensions of the family is given when the ceremony takes place in the house, as can be done if desired. The ceremony takes place on the section of floor where the Household Godling is worshipped and is much the same as at the spring, except that cooked foods, including fish, crab, and chicken are placed on the plates. The *pitri* are invited to come and partake by pouring a line of water along the entrance hall to the place of sacrifice and saying, "Lo, *pitri,* please come in." When the ceremony is over, water is poured in the other direction and they are politely asked to leave. The tone is courteous but not overly respectful and surely not fearful. They are more like ordinary living members of the family than *bai*.

Men who do not ask Brahmans to come and conduct their pujas are aware that their method of worship is different. But they do not feel it is wrong. They regard it as the more traditional way, one which is appropriate for persons who are not wealthy or well-educated.

6

Kin

Lineage

THE MAGAR subtribes, such as the Thapas and the Ranas, each are divided into many large clans whose members are widely scattered. In Banyan Hill, among the men, three Thapa clans are represented and two Rana clans. All of the Headman's lineage belong to the Sinjali clan of Thapas, but Bom Bahadur is a Makkim Thapa and Havildar Santa Prased a Sunari. Om Bahadur is a Sinjali Thapa, but not at all closely related to the Headman's lineage of Sinjalis. All of Shri Ram's lineage belong to the Lungeli clan of Ranas. Bir Bahadur, who is also a Rana, belongs to the Hiski clan. Magars who belong to the same clan cannot marry; otherwise any Magar can marry any other, including members of his own subtribe. Regulation of marriage is the major function of clans, and beyond this, clan membership is of slight significance. Members of the same clan believe they all are descended in the male line from a shared (but now unknown) male ancestor; clan ancestors, it is felt, are related through male links to some extremely remote progenitor of the whole Magar tribe.

The Sinjali Thapas of the Headman's lineage all are descended from a Sinjali named Nareshwar, who lived about two hundred years ago. When his sons married they built houses in Banyan Hill near their father. His daughters, however, moved to live with their husbands who stayed near *their* fathers. The pattern of more or less stationary sons and moving daughters has created the spatial clustering of Sinjali families in Kutumsa and Darkang.

The Sinjalis of the Headman's lineage share male ancestors with other Sinjali families who live in nearby hamlets. These ancestors, who are more remote than Nareshwar, lived from ten to fourteen generations ago. The Adamara headman was a Sinjali relative of this kind, but neither he nor the other neighboring Sinjalis considered themselves members of the Headman's lineage. They had "hived off," and were separate now from the Banyan Hill lineage in both a

59

geographical and a ritual sense. It is probable that in Dirgha Singh we can see the initial step of just such a process.

The test for lineage membership is common pollution at the time of birth or death and shared observances of taboos. The headman of Banyan Hill normally did two pujas every day. But when a daughter was born to Dev Bahadur, his lineage brother in Darkang, he refrained from doing his pujas or worship of any kind for eleven days, the period of pollution caused by birth. The same taboo on worship was observed by all other members of his lineage: by his brothers; the Havildar Major and his cousin brother, Dirgha Singh; and the women who lived near Dev Bahadur. The Thapa families who had hived off did not believe themselves to be polluted by this birth and hence did not feel it necessary to refrain from worship.

A similar communal pollution is acquired by lineage members when a death occurs. For the death of an adult, the period of pollution is thirteen days; besides refraining from worship, lineage members also are expected to refrain from eating any salt. A child who dies before it is named pollutes only the mother; only she must observe funeral taboos. The death of a child who is named, but less than three years old, pollutes only the parents. Any child older than this, for purposes of funeral taboo, is considered an adult; his death affects the whole lineage.

If one notes carefully what family members do not eat salt during a period of death pollution, it will be seen that daughters are exempt. This is true even if it is their own father who has died. In this context, daughters are not regarded as members of their fathers' or their brothers' lineage, even though they are not married. Later, when a daughter marries and goes to live in her husband's home, she becomes a member of his lineage and will observe the same taboos that he does. But her daughters will be exempt, just as she was when she was in her father's home.

In composition most lineages, as defined by men who follow common ritual observances, correspond with a group of men called *hukdar*. The word carries the sense of "one who has a title to or an interest in." To determine who his *hukdar* are, a man counts up six ascending generations, from his father to his paternal grandfather, to this man's father, and so on for six generations. All men who are descended through male links from the ancestor arrived at in this way are his *hukdar*. According to this way of reckoning, all living males in the Headman's lineage in Banyan Hill are *hukdar* to one another. The Rana men of Chepte consider themselves a lineage but are not certain whether all are *hukdar* or not. They have lost track of the genealogical links by which they could decide.

If a man dies without sons or without having previously willed some of his property to a religious institution or to a daughter, all of his estate, after payment of debts, is apportioned among the *hukdar*. Those most closely related to him receive a larger share than those who are more distantly related.

Generally, men who die do have surviving sons, and the *hukdar* do not have any claim. But this is not always the case. The father-in-law of Bom Bahadur had no sons. Before he died, he left a will giving half his estate, as he was entitled to do, to his daughter. The *hukdar* have no claim on this property, and Bom Bahadur's sons can inherit it. This right is regarded as recompense to Bom Bahadur and his sons for looking after the mother-in-law and helping manage her deceased husband's farm. The *hukdar* do have a claim on the remaining half of the estate, a portion that Bom Bahadur's mother-in-law may enjoy as long as she lives but not sell without their permission. After her death, the *hukdar* will claim some of this estate to pay for her funeral. When she married, she became part of their lineage and they, not her son-in-law nor her daughter, who belongs to her husband's lineage, are responsible for carrying out her last rites. The decision about the amount it is proper to spend on a funeral usually is made in consultation with the headmen and other respected men of the community. Although the *hukdar* legally have a right to the remainder of the property, they do not always avail themselves of it, especially when the daughter, as is true in Bom Bahadur's household, has many sons. This is an indication that pressure on land in this section of the hills is not yet extreme.

An individual's *hukdar* group consists of males who have *different* rights in commonly owned property depending upon the number of genealogical links between them and a deceased person. In contrast, some lineages and sections of lineages hold *equal* rights in property on a common share basis. The Chepte lineage jointly owns a field of irrigated rice, and each family year by year takes turns using it. Each of the two Banyan Hill lineages holds separate fields where thatch can be cut, and lineage families are allowed to cut thatch there year by year in rotation. Lineages also have a responsibility for widows. For a year following the death of a husband or a son, an indigent widow who has no other males in her family can turn to the lineage for help in obtaining labor. It is the custom for a lineage to provide one man for one day from each house to assist in whatever tasks she designates. Her only responsibility is to provide light refreshment, such as beer and parched maize. The whole Chepte lineage shares equally in wood lots and grazing lands. In the Headman's lineage, sharing of this kind of property has been divided into three segments: the Headman and his brothers, the Havildar Major and Dirgha Singh, and Dev Bahadur and his closest relatives at that end of the community. Each of these three groups have joint interests in wood lots and grazing lands, but none of them shares irrigated rice plots.

At the time of a funeral, a deceased man's sons, closest lineage brothers, and occasionally the husband of a daughter or sister take turns carrying his bier to the riverside. When a wife dies, her sons and her husband's lineage brothers, but not the husband, carry out this task.

The rule that a wife leaves her parents and a husband remains near his creates neighborhoods consisting of families linked together in a lineage, or a portion of a lineage. The neighborhood tie, strengthened by the lineage tie, finds expression in cooperative activities. Maila Ba's wives join the wife and daughters of the Havildar Major in carrying manure to the fields prior to maize planting, and the Havildar Major is asked to come and help weigh and divide the Headman's jewelry and metal utensils when he is partitioning his estate among his sons. The ties of neighborhood and lineal kinship also are expressed by food borrowing or communal use of one particularly good grindstone. These ties are further demonstrated when the Havildar's eldest boy, who is fifteen, comes in the evening to sit on the porch with Maila Ba and share his hookah.

People closest bound by ties of kinship and neighborhood sometimes will feel hostility, and it is a hostility that is all the more bitter because of the intensity of association. This was true of the relation between Maila Ba and Kanchha Ba. Kanchha Ba, who had given up liquor, tobacco, and meat, was openly critical of his older brother who had not. The tension between the two families burst out one day when Kanchha Ba's goats got into Maila Ba's wheat field. When he came to retrieve them, attracted by the shouting of his brother and his brother's eldest wife, he was reminded loudly by both that more attention to watching his goats and less attention to religion and to criticism of the older acceptable customs of others would be greatly appreciated.

There was much solidarity among the members of the Chepte lineage. All lived near one another; all had roughly the same economic status and values, especially in the sphere of religion. It is possible, too, that they were drawn closer together by feelings of antagonism for the Headman, who frequently turned to this group for free labor.

In the Headman's lineage, there were three major fissions that followed lines of genealogical segmentation. There was little cooperation or friendly interchange between the Headman and his brothers as a group and the Darkang group. Darkang's closest ties were outside their lineage with Brahmans and with Magar relatives in the nearby community of Adamara. The third segment of the Headman's lineage was represented by the Havildar Major and his cousin brother, Dirgha Singh. Dirgha and the Havildar were not close, but the Havildar was treated almost like a true brother rather than a somewhat distant collateral by the Headman and his brothers. He was even invited to participate in their intimate family conferences. When the Headman's present wife objected to having the *pewa* property of one of his former, deceased wives divided among the deceased wife's children alone, the Headman one afternoon called his brothers and the Havildar together. They sat in a row with their backs against his buffalo shed husking corn and finally coming to agreement among themselves that the children of the present wife did not have a true claim.

There are examples of a man's acting like a lineage brother and in some ways being regarded as one, even though he is too distantly related to observe the pollutional and ritual aspects of lineage membership. Sita Devi, whose husband was in Assam, and Jag Maya, the widow, turned to the Adamara headman as if he were a member of their lineage. They were friendly with his three unmarried daughters, and although he lived about a quarter of a mile away, there were no houses between theirs and his so that he was one of their closest neighbors. Also, he belonged to the same Sinjali clan as their husbands, and although he was a very distant relative, they called him by the kin term for grandfather. There was much more in common between Sita Devi and the Adamara headman than among her and any of her nearby adult lineage males except Dev Bahadur. Both were attracted to young people, and their houses frequently were used for singing. Both followed the older Magar customs and enjoyed meat and liquor. A service Dev Bahadur performed for Sita Devi, was to butcher her pig for the Dasain festival. As part of the butchering, he dipped his hands in the blood and made three bloody handprints, one on each side of her door and a third above it, in order to help keep away witches and their evil influence.

In-laws

Besides the lineage, there are two other sets of relatives that are very important to each Banyan Hill family. These are persons who have become relatives as a result of marriages. They are the in-laws, or affines. It will be remembered that the Headman's lineage regarded Shri Ram's lineage as the group to whom they gave their sisters and daughters as wives. It is not true that the Sinjalis gave all their sisters and daughters to this group, but they do give some (Dhem Bahadur's mother, for example), and it will be useful in explaining Magar social structure to consider for a moment that all girls from the Headman's lineage do marry men from Shri Ram's lineage in Chepte.

Magars speak of daughters and sisters who have left home and married as *cheli-beti.* They speak of the men they marry, and the lineage brothers of these men, as *kutumba.* More broadly, they sometimes refer to their married daughters or sisters, the husbands of these women, the husbands' lineage brothers, and even the village where they all live as *kutumba.* If all girls from Darkang and Kutumsa went to Chepte when they married, everyone in the Headman's lineage would refer to Chepte and the people there as their *kutumba.* Girls always refer to their home, their father's lineage, and their natal village as *maita.*

Magars say that when they have something auspicious to celebrate they call the *cheli-beti,* but when there is some inauspicious work to be done, they call their husbands, the *kutumba.* This is not strictly true, because the *kutumba* and *cheli-beti* both help with funerals. What they are thinking of are the festivals such as Dasain, when their married daughters return home with their families, and of funerals, when their husbands must be called for such duties as the chicken sacrifice, which only they can perform.

If the point of view is shifted to Chepte, it can be seen that the Headman's lineage is a wife-giving group. Furthermore, if all girls came from this lineage, it is apparent that every boy who marries is taking a girl from the same lineage that his mother came from. In some cases, he might actually marry the daughter of his mother's brother, who is called *mama.* When a Magar talks about his marriage rule this is one of the things he says: "We prefer to marry our *mama's* daughter." If *mama* does not have a daughter, he says he prefers any girl younger than he, who is a daughter of *mama's* lineage. In this way, all the unmarried girls of the right age in the Headman's lineage become *potential* wives of a boy in Chepte. Since they are potential wives, he feels free to joke with them about sex and to touch them very freely. In this idealized picture of Magar social structure, the Chepte boy always would refer to Darkang and Kutumsa as *mamali* —the lineage and general village area where his mother's brother lives.

Marrying *mama's* daughter is a preference and is not the same as the strict rule that Magars cannot marry father's sister's daughters. One reason this rule is important to Magars is that it distinguishes them from tribes such as the Gurungs and Thakalis, who do permit and even prefer, such marriages; in addition they also permit or prefer marriages with *mama's* daughter. This means that a Gurung who lived in Chepte might take a girl from the Headman's lineage as his wife, and in the next generation he might give his daughter to someone in the Head-man's lineage as a bride. The Magars of the Headman's lineage would express their objection to this situation by saying that the girls in Chepte belong to the "milk side." Because they have Sinjali mothers they have "drunk Sinjali milk" and therefore are unsuitable wives for Sinjali men.

Of course this picture of relations with in-laws is not the actual picture. It is true that some Sinjali girls do go to Chepte as wives, and it would be possible for a Chepte boy to marry the real daughter of his Sinjali mother's brother. But of fifty-three recent marriages recorded in Banyan Hill, only about one quarter were to a real mother's brother's daughter or even to a girl who was born into the lineage of the real mother's brother. There is merely a tendency to take girls from the mother's natal lineage or from the girl's point of view, to marry a boy from the lineage of her father's sister's husband. Otherwise, Magars find whatever girls they can who do not belong to their clan and who do not come from lineages where girls of their own lineage recently have gone as wives. Thus, instead of a marriage pattern that links the Headman's lineage with only two villages— Chepte, where it sends girls and some other village, from which it gets wives— there is a marriage pattern that connects the lineages of Banyan Hill with several other places. And a high proportion of the wives come from lineages other than the ones their husband's mothers came from.

Although the Magar marriage network does include many different places and lineages, they are not widely scattered. Of forty-six in-coming wives, eighteen came from within the thum itself; twenty-two came from villages a mile to five miles from the thum; and five from villages six to fifteen miles distant. Only one girl came from a village over sixteen miles away, a distance that represents a walk of a day and a half.

Despite the fact that the Magar preference for marrying a mother's broth-er's daughter or a girl belonging to a mother's brother's lineage is more evident in the breach than in the observance, with a resulting multiplex marriage pattern, it can be regarded as a relationship of girl giving or girl receiving between whole lineages, rather than between individual families. This is how the Magars tend to think of it.

The reason can be seen if we understand tendencies that come into play at a time when a boy is the first one in his lineage to marry a girl from another vil-lage. This girl's family, his *susural,* is part of a lineage. Even though the group may be split into more or less antagonistic segments, like those of Kutumsa and

Darkang, it continues to be thought of as a single unit. This is so primarily because of joint interests in land and ideas such as those of shared pollution at birth
and death. In marriage, the unity of the lineage is acted out when the bride's father, plus all the other men she calls "father"—her father's lineage brothers—
one after another put tikka on the groom's forehead, jointly accepting him as an
in-law. To this unitary tendency in a lineage is added a tendency to regard any
lineage that has given one daughter away in marriage as a wife-giving group, just
like the mother's brother's lineage. The tendency for the whole lineage to appear
as a source of potential wives is seen when the newly married groom begins to
joke freely, not just with the younger sisters of his bride, but with all the girls in
her lineage who are younger than he. They have become potential wives.

This tendency for the new bride's lineage to be drawn into the category
of mother's brother's lineage, even though it is not, is not surprising when we
realize that in another generation it could very well become such a lineage. It
would be quite possible for the son of the present groom to marry the daughter
of his mother's brother, or some girl from his mother's brother's lineage; in this
case the lineage which was *susural* to his father would be *mamali* to him.

The effects of these tendencies are not limited to the groom. When his
younger brother and young friends from his lineage go to a songfest in the new
wife's village, they joke with the girls there. These girls are potential wives because a lineage mate has married one of their "sisters." But it goes further than
joking. The adults in the groom's lineage now feel that they have some right to
look in this village for marriageable girls for their sons and that the families
there have some obligation to provide them with wives. They do not feel they
have as much right to expect this as they would in the next generation, but the
right is well enough recognized on both sides so that a single marriage in a new
place sometimes begins a "run" on girls from that particular lineage and village.

From the bride's side, the groom's village becomes a source of possible
kutumba. There are families with no daughters and thus no real *kutumba* to come
and perform essential services at the time of a funeral or marriage. If there were
such a family in the new bride's lineage, it would feel it could ask the groom, or
one of his lineage "brothers," to come and act as *kutumba*.

It is this blotter-like spreading of affinal relationships that tends to exclude any lineage among Magars that has received a girl from becoming a possible giver of wives. This was the case with Chepte—to a degree. For here again
we are faced with contrary tendencies that give rise to the tensions and ambiguities of actual social intercourse. The difficulty that arose was expressed in the
form of a question: How many in the Chepte lineage had absorbed the Sinjali
"milk" and how much? The question arose when the Headman's eldest son married his second wife, the daughter of Shri Ram. The tendencies to consider Shri
Ram's lineage as a wife-receiving lineage, or *kutumba,* were strong. There was
the tradition. There were also recent marriages. The Headman's sister had gone
there as a wife to an uncle of the bride, and the groom's grandfather's sister was
the mother of the bride's grandfather. All this strongly suggested *kutumba.* But
it was argued by the Headman's son and Shri Ram himself that the Sinjali milk

had been diluted by the marriage of the bride's grandfather and father to non-Sinjali girls. Still, people were disturbed and the reason was that their expectations were confused. From the point of view of the Headman's lineage the question was whether Shri Ram's lineage was now one in which one could joke with the girls and consider them potential wives, or was it the place where one turned for assistance at the time of a funeral? Was it *mamali* or *kutumba?* The trouble was that it was something of both; even though the situation was being lived with and accepted, the existence of this ambiguity did cause a little uneasiness.

Ritual Friends and Siblings

Some relatives are acquired at birth and others at marriage. A third group is acquired voluntarily. These are ritual friends and ritually adopted brothers and sisters. A ritual friend unvaryingly belongs to a caste other than one's own, and only persons of the same sex perform the ritual that establishes such a relationship. The situation is different with ritual brothers or sisters. Here the link is between members of the same caste and is formed between persons of the opposite sex.

The circumstances that lead to a ritual friendship are various. Often the decision to become ritual friends will be made as a result of a mutual and spontaneous welling-up of affection. This may occur after a very brief acquaintance. Young men are especially prone to find ritual friends in this way, and a common occasion is an all-night songfest that brings young people together from a number of different villages. Young men going to and from army service find ritual friends when they stop to eat and drink in trailside hostels or when they go to villages other than their own to visit relatives. For both boys and girls, the cooperative work group, which brings young people of different castes together, is a context in which the desire for establishing such a bond springs up. Sometimes young people are brought together by parents. The parents may be good friends but may not have established the bond formally. As an expression of their mutual regard, they encourage the young people to become ritual friends.

There are occasions when a person desires ritual friendship more as a means to an end than as an end in itself. One woman, whose own mother was dead and who had no close female relatives in her natal village who could fill the status of mother, chose as a ritual friend a Gurung girl whose mother she liked very much. Since girls who become ritual friends become sisters, the Magar woman in this way acquired a mother and a new natal household. Some ritual friends are made on the advice of the astrologer. This is more common among the girls and women of Banyan Hill than it is among the boys and men. Of twenty Banyan Hill men who were questioned, only one said he had entered into the relationship to improve his stars. But of the twenty-seven women who discussed their ritual friendships, something over one fifth said they had acquired the friend because the astrologer had advised them to obtain one belonging to a lower caste than theirs. The belief is that sickness or bad luck results from a poor configuration of controlling stars. This configuration often can be improved through ritual friendship with persons of a lower caste.

Beliefs about whether there are any harmful results for the person chosen for this reason are not uniform. Some say that no harm results and others speak about transferring illness or bad luck to the other. One does not tell why one is seeking a ritual friend, and the person who is sought after is not supposed to ask questions about motives. As a result, some ambiguity inheres in the institution. This could be seen when the Headman's daughter acquired a ritual friend. She went to bathe in the Kali Gandaki during one of the religious festival occasions. She was bathing apart from her parents and was approached by a Brahman woman and her daughter. The mother suggested that the two girls go through the ceremony that would make them ritual friends. Despite a little reluctance on the part of the Headman's daughter, the girls did this. When the Headman's daughter told her parents what had happened, they scolded her. They said they were certain she had been selected because the Brahman girl's stars needed strengthening, and they were afraid the relation might prove to be an inauspicious one.

Dev Bahadur's wife and her ritual friend established the relationship in a very simple way. She and a Tailor girl had been close friends and had been addressing each other as "ritual girl friend." One night when they and other young people had gathered to sing together, they decided to recognize the relationship formally. They merely sat opposite each other and each placed a silver rupee and a *pice* on a piece of banana leaf and set it before their friend. After picking up the coins, the girls completed the ceremony by rising and bowing to one another.

In a more elaborate ceremony, such as one that made ritual friends of the Adamara headman's daughter and a Brahman widow nineteen years old, a Brahman was present and the girls participated together in a simple puja in the courtyard of the Brahman girl's parents' house. They exchanged gifts, which included (from each girl) flowers, a mirror, eye paint, a cloth purse with money in it, and some sugar candy. Each girl was accompanied by her brothers, and following the ceremony the whole group was given a meal by parents of the Brahman girl. This was an instance of ritual friendship formed for ulterior ends, since the connection was formed on the advice of the officiating Brahman as a way of improving the Brahman girl's stars. The two girls were such strangers to one another that during the ceremony and the festivities following they were too shy to speak to one another.

Once the tie of ritual friendship has been formed, each of the participants acquires a whole new set of relatives. He addresses each of them as his friends would, calling his friends mother, "mother" (*ama*) and so on. When he discusses these kinsmen, he makes it clear that they are ritual relatives, not real ones. The word for a man's ritual friend is *mit*. When speaking to his *mit,* he would use the term *ama;* when talking about this woman to someone else, he would describe her as his *mit-ama.*

As a rule, ritual friendships reach a peak of intensity right after they are formed and then tend to lapse. In the early stage, there is much reciprocal visiting. In time this gives way to a visit a year, and finally to chatting briefly together whenever they chance to meet, which may be very seldom. In some cases the relationship may persist across generations. The Havildar Major's father was a close ritual friend of a Metalworker. Many years after the death of the Havildar's father, his Metalworker ritual uncle continued to pay a call at least once a year. He generally brought an iron sickle he had made and received in return some millet, a crop he was unable to grow in his own village. The utility of this relationship was one reason it persisted, and doubtless many of the ritual friendships based merely on a need for improved stars or on youthful affection diminish in intensity and die out because they are based on nothing more lasting and substantial. Analysis of persons involved in all kinds of buying, selling, and borrowing and loaning transactions in Banyan Hill reveals that the relation of ritual friendship has almost no direct involvement here. Nor does it play a very important part in providing security when traveling. Most ritual friends live within Pandera Thum or in nearby thums.

Ritual friends who are on visiting terms generally drop in at one another's houses on one or two of the festival days that occur throughout the year. Dasain is especially apt to bring ritual friends together. Men and boys do not carry food to each other's houses, but girls always do. The friend rarely stays for more than one or two meals, and during his visit he often will be found chatting or napping on the verandah. A young people's songfest in a nearby town sometimes will be an occasion for a longer stay.

Jag Maya, the widow in Darkang, is the only person in Banyan Hill who has ritual brothers. One of the men, a Magar, was in the army long ago with her father. He was much younger than Jag Maya's father and used to receive tikka from him, as if he were his son. When Jag Maya's father died she had no one to receive tikka from at Dasain, and she went to this man, whom she regarded as a brother. He had no sisters, and in turn came to her for tikka as a brother on Brother-Worship Day. This exchange of tikka as brother and sister established their relationship, which on the brother's side was expanded to include his younger brother, his only other living sibling. Both men come to help their ritual sister, especially at harvest times. It is believed that a ritual brother will continue to be one's brother throughout seven rebirths.

Dasain and the Ritual Renewal of Kin Ties

The great festival of the Nepali year is Dasain, which in India is called Dasera. In Banyan Hill, Dasain was used loosely to refer to a period that included other festivals as well as the one that strictly would be called Dasain. In 1961, this general period of ceremonial began on the day after the dark of the moon in the month of Aswin (September 19) and ended two days after the dark of the moon in the month of Kartik (November 10). The maize had been harvested and the rice and millet stood ripe in the fields. Harvesting of both these crops began during the festival and intensified as soon as it ended.

Families make preparations for this festival long in advance. It is a time for new clothing and shopkeepers lay in large extra supplies of cloth. A Tailor family comes to the Deorali bazaar to work on newly purchased cloth, and other Tailors go from house to house. Stills for making liquor are set up, and those who do not make liquor themselves go about trying to purchase it. The walls of the houses are newly painted with a mixture of water, cowdung and orange-colored mud, and the wooden windows and the door frames are painted black with color obtained from boiled roots or the insides of used-up dry cell batteries.

Dasain emphasizes and weaves together a great many facets of community life. Above all it is a time when important kinship bonds are renewed and, as it were, acted out in a context of ritual and festivity. The ritual drama of kinship renewal begins on the tenth day of the Dasain festival. This is Tikka Day, which is heralded in the early morning by shotgun firing from houses where there are guns. On Tikka Day, the focus is on the lineage and on the respect due age. The central rite is placing rice mixed with curd and usually also with red coloring on the forehead of a younger person by his elder. The ceremony generally begins within each family; then the family members, or someone to represent them, obtain tikka from an elder who represents the lineage as a whole or some segment of it.

In Chepte the eldest member of Padam Bahadur's family is his mother. Tikka-giving began in the morning with the old lady squatting on a woven straw mat on the porch. Beside her sat a brass bowl of mixed curd and colored rice plus a dish of copper coins, and a basket with cut sage and some barley sprouts that had been planted on the first day of Dasain and had been forced to grow rapidly in the warm kitchen. Padam squated before her, and using both hands she pressed tikka onto his forehead five times and then put some of the auspicious barley sprouts mixed with sage behind his ear. Padam leaned down and touched his mother's feet with his hands and forehead, in a gesture of respect and thanks for the well-wishing that the tikka, sage, and barley represented. While he was doing this obeisance, his son tried vainly to fire the family shotgun, an ancient muzzle-loading matchlock.

The next to receive tikka was the second son, Teg Bahadur, who lived in the adjacent house. By rights the third person to receive tikka should have been the wife of Padam, but their young daughter, who was at an age when she had just lost all her front teeth, was so eager to receive it that she was permitted to come next. After giving the tikka, her grandmother did not place barley and sage behind her ears. This is not the custom for girls. Instead, as a daughter of the house and lineage she received a few copper coins. The special goddess-like ritual status of an unmarried daughter of the family and lineage also was shown when the grandmother, instead of receiving obeisance, touched her forehead to her granddaughter's feet. The girl responded only by pressing a portion of her shawl between her palms, holding it before her face, and bending forward from the waist.

The wife of Padam was next; she was followed by the second son's wife, who brought a gift of pork and liquor. She brought this into the house before receiving tikka; as always, to show her respect to the family of her husband's elder brother, she touched her forehead to the threshold. After she received tikka, she went to the wife of her elder brother and touched her forehead to her feet. (She and her husband's elder brother show respect for each other not by touching, but by avoiding contact.)

Since Padam Bahadur's mother also was the oldest person in the whole lineage, representatives from all families came to receive tikka from her. It is true that the oldest male in the lineage, and its focal elderly male, was Shri Ram. But he was younger than Padam Bahadur's mother, and fell into the category of son. Normally a person having this relationship would have come to her for tikka. Shri Ram, however, felt the importance of being the most elderly male and in temperament was inclined to be crotchety. To humor him, Padam Bahadur's mother, who was an easy-going old lady, went to his house and gave him tikka there. The scene at Shri Ram's was similar to the one at Padam Bahadur's house. Children from all the lineage houses, plus adult representatives from most of them, came to squat before him and have him press rice onto their foreheads three times. When he gave tikka he added a blessing, saying, "May you be healthy. May you have no enemy. Even if you get old, may no harm come to you when you walk about."

Those who give tikka are expected to provide a meal for the persons who have received it. In the case of a family with many members, the obligation, it is understood, covers only one or two of its representatives. The meals are spread out over a number of days and consist mainly of rice, pork, and liquor. Not everyone who comes for tikka brings pork and liquor as a gift, but many do. Padam Bahadur's mother, for example, in addition to the pork and liquor from her son, Teg, received pork from two lineage grandnephews, pork and liquor from her daughter and her husband, sweet fried bread from a lineage son who was sick and could not come for tikka, and pork from a lineage niece and her husband. On Tikka Day, she sent pork and liquor via her youngest grandson to Teg and his wife, and while there the grandson received tikka from his uncle and stayed to eat his tikka meal.

During Dasain, the Headman's lineage reveals its division. In Darkang, Dev Bahadur's mother is the oldest person, and she plays a role there that is similar to that played by Padam Bahadur's mother in Chepte. Dev Bahadur is the oldest male and he functions like Shri Ram. In the other part of the lineage, the focal figure is the Headman; representatives from all the families in his lineage go to his house to receive tikka, including representatives from Darkang houses. The tendency toward fission is evident in the patterns of reciprocal visiting. Young people from the Headman's section of the lineage should go to receive tikka from Dev Bahadur's mother, but they do not. Most of their tikka visits, and hence meals, are confined to the Headman's sector, excluding Dirgha Singh. And it is mostly children who are sent from Darkang to the Headman for tikka. The adults prefer to go to the Adamara headman. They can bring him gifts of pork and liquor, whereas bananas, melons, or cucumbers are the acceptable gifts for the vegetarian Banyan Hill headman. Likewise, the meal they receive from the Adamara headman is the traditional rice, pork, and liquor, while at the Headman's it is rice, curds, and vegetables.

When sisters and daughters return to their natal homes to receive tikka from their father, their mother, and other elders of the lineage, they usually bring their husbands and children with them. Tikka Day is an occasion when ties between in-law homes are reaffirmed. If the sister or daughter herself cannot visit her parents, her husband usually will go, as Padam Bahadur did when he went to receive tikka from his wife's ritual mother. It is customary to carry meat and liquor to the wife's natal home. Since men find it embarrassing to carry such gifts, if possible they take an older child with them, especially an older daughter. In Banyan Hill during the tikka-giving period it was the exceptional family that was not visited by sisters, daughters, and their husbands and children, most of them from villages outside of Banyan Hill. And it was the exceptional family that did not send a group, or at least a member to visit the wife's natal home.

Tikka Day emphasizes ties to elderly people within one's own or one's natal lineage. The tendency is toward crossing of generations. The festival that follows very closely on Dasain and is thought of as part of the same general period of visiting, feasting, and religious observance, is Tivahar. In Tivahar, the kinship ties that are stressed are those between brother and sister, ties within the same generation. During the autumn period of Dasain, there are two important dark periods of the moon. One, *pitri aunsi,* falls just before Dasain and, as we have seen, marks a time when ancestral spirits are fed and honored. The subsequent *aunsi* falls during Tivahar. When the mother or father is alive, married daughters and sisters usually are invited to come and eat rice in their natal home on both *aunsis*. When the mother and father are dead, one may ask them for both *aunsis,* but it is equally appropriate to invite them for only one. If the girls or a representative from their family cannot come on one of the *aunsis,* rice and other foods will be sent to their house—a gift known as "brother's rice." On Brother-Worship Day during the Tivahar *aunsi,* unmarried sisters still in the natal home give tikka to their brothers; married sisters invite their brothers to come to their house for tikka and for a feast. It is believed that giving tikka to the brother on this occasion prolongs his life. If for some reason the brother cannot come to the sister's house, she will go to his.

When Padam and Teg Bahadur's sister came to their house (they were unable to go to hers), she carried enough food and liquor for all members in both brothers' houses. It was the food she would have fed them if they had come to her own house. She also brought strings of flowers that she fastened as a sign of good omen over the doors of each brother's house, and under each garland she placed a tikka made of rice. Her brothers squatted before her in a rice-straw mat while she placed a tikka on the forehead of each. The tikkas sisters give their brothers on this occasion are three small upright rectangles, each of a different color. Padam's and Teg's sister had bought yellow, blue, and red powder in the bazaar. She mixed the colors with water, and to get them on evenly she made a stencil out of banana leaf and drew in the tikkas with a bit of straw. After each tikka had been drawn, she placed a garland around the brothers' neck. They thanked her, and each honored her by placing his forehead on her feet. Following the brothers' tikka, she gave tikka to their wives, although without flower garlands, and then to Padam's daughters. Finally she helped Padam's youngest daughter draw appropriate tikkas on the little girl's own brothers' foreheads.

In Tivahar, Jag Maya, the widow with ritual brothers, usually goes to their house laden with food and liquor. They find it difficult to get away from the demands of farm work long enough to come to her house.

Om Bahadur has a Metalworker as an active ritual friend. Since the friend is Untouchable, he cannot invite Om's wife, his "sister," to come to his house to eat during *aunsi*. Instead, he sends her uncooked rice, spices, meat, and liquor. In Tivahar, on Brother-Worship Day, she invites him to come and eat. She cannot feed him in the house, so she makes a very large leaf plate and places in it a number of smaller leaf plates filled with various kinds of food. The whole spread is sealed with a leaf cover. The Metalworker "brother" eats it squatting in the courtyard; Om's wife points out with amusement that since he is shy, he does not take off the leaf cover to look and see what the food is but instead discreetly reaches underneath, taking only a bit at a time.

7

Caste

Service Castes

WITH THE COMING of civilization to the Middle East, a way of life came into being unlike anything that had preceded it. This way of life would not have been possible without the new techniques of cattle-drawn plows and irrigation, for they made it possible for farmers to grow more than enough to support themselves and their families. Some of this extra food, in turn, could be used to free some families from the necessity of growing all their own food. They could specialize in occupations other than farming—in metal working, cloth manufacture, religious speculation. In India, the tendency toward specialization of labor became part of the caste system, a system that spread to the hills of Nepal and deeply affected life there, especially in the more southerly portion where Banyan Hill is located. We will describe other aspects of the caste system as it affects families in Banyan Hill but will begin by noting how it provides families with special services that they themselves do not perform. From this point of view, we can see that the rules of caste reserve certain occupations almost without exception to certain families and provide shared understandings about compensation for the work that is done. Basically, it is a matter of exchanging a skill for food.

TAILORS

One of the groups in Pandera Thum with a special skill, is a group of Tailor families. There are thirteen households in all, and they are clustered together just under the highest point of the ridge on which Pandera Thum is located. From here, during the winter months, they go out into the hamlets of this thum and other nearby thums and sew clothing. Six of these families include the Magar farmers of Banyan Hill among their clientele. This provides for all Banyan Hill families except one, a family that uses a Tailor from a nearby village in a different thum. Of the seven Tailor families who sew for the Banyan Hill Magars, all but one now have sewing machines. These machines and the other equipment that the Tailors use provide an excellent illustration of how wide a portion of the world their mountain hamlet can draw upon. Two of the machines were purchased in a town near the Indian border, but a third came from Calcutta; one all the way from Malaya. (It was brought back by a Tailor who had served there in the British army.)

During the winter months, two members of the family, often a man and his wife, set out for the home of one of their clients. The man carries his machine on his back, supported by a tumpline. They take their meals at the client's house, and unless they wish to sit in the sun to keep warm, will do their work in a corner of the verandah. They are given a rice-straw mat to sit on; if they have stayed all day, when they leave for home at night, they are given a pound of uncooked rice to take with them for the evening meal. The man works the machine and the woman does the hand sewing. Two or three days generally is enough time to complete the work needed by a single family. The relationship between a Tailor family and its client family tends to persist from generation to generation, although there is no strong resistance to making changes if either side wishes.

The Tailors sew a variety of clothes, such as jumpers (for girls), shirts, vests, shorts, and underpants (for men). But the items most in demand are blouses for both men and women. A Tailor who works for a regular client supplies his own thread; if asked to make a man's cap—usually one for each man in the family is required—he also supplies the cloth. In addition to the meals provided the Tailor when he spends the day at a client's house, he is given grain on a piecework basis. The amount given varies from family to family. The Havildar Major provides an example of the amount of work done by the Tailor and the amount paid him by an average family. His Tailor came on three occasions in 1961, in Magh (January-February), Asar (June–July), and during Dasain (October). In all he made ten shirts for the Havildar and his three sons; two blouses for the Havildar's wife; two blouses for his daughter; three vests for the boys; and six caps. On one occasion, the Tailor sat all day at the Havildar's and was fed. On the other two he came to pick up the cloth and worked on the items at home. He was then paid according to the following formula: for six pieces sewed at home, three pounds of rice; for four pieces, two pounds; and for two pieces, one pound.

Except for Dil Maya, all the households in Banyan Hill are regular clients of one of the Tailor families. This means that at certain times during the year, the Tailor family has a right to expect a payment of field produce. It also means that they can visit their client on various festival occasions and receive either food and drink or some grain. The number, kind, and amount of these payments vary with the wealth and generosity of the client. To establish a bench mark at one end of the scale we can note what Maila Ba paid, since he is both well-to-do and generous. Following the spring harvest he gave his Tailor about eighteen pounds of paddy. At this time, many families give millet. Though millet is a valued grain, paddy is still more desirable because it must be grown on irrigated fields. As a rule the Tailors and other specialists do not have such fields. They must look to their wealthier clients for much of their rice supply. Following the fall harvest, Maila Ba gave his Tailor approximately twenty-four pounds of maize. These are the major yearly payments and are called *bali*. He also made two additional payments. One is called *chaiti-sauni* for the months of the spring and fall harvests. For the *chaiti* (March–April) payment he gave about six pounds of paddy and gave the same amount for the *sauni* (July–August). For the second kind of payment, known as the wheat share, he gave approximately three pounds of wheat. If he had grown any unirrigated or "dry" rice, he also would have given a dry rice share.

For most farmers, the usual *bali* payment consists of millet and maize, but in somewhat lesser amounts than were paid by Maila Ba. Only Bikram, who is not as generous as most and was feeling somewhat pinched financially, failed to give something for spring and fall *bali*. There was much more variation in the other payments. Seven farms paid *chaiti-sauni* and wheat share, only four paid dry rice share. The well-to-do farmers paid the *chaiti-sauni;* it also was paid by poorer farmers who had had a good year and wished to be generous and well-thought of. The wheat and dry rice payments generally were a reflection of whether or not the farmer planted those two crops.

It is clear that payments of this kind are flexible, personal, and dependent upon a number of variables. An important variable not yet mentioned is whether or not the specialist makes the effort to come and ask for payments at the time when he is most apt to be given them. Wheat yields, for example, generally are small. The specialist who comes right after the threshing is more apt to get some than if he were to come a few months later. It is much the same for a payment not usually regarded as among the regular payments—a bundle of rice straw from the threshing floor. The specialist who takes the trouble to go and ask will almost always be given some. Much depends on the specialist's needs and the time at his disposal.

The patterns of payments on festival occasions resemble the pattern of harvest payments. The same variables are significant. If one were to list the festival occasions on which a farmer would give something to a specialist if he happened to appear and ask, the list would include at least fourteen festivals. Actually, no family would feed a specialist or give him grain on all fourteen of these occasions. To take Maila Ba again as an example, on eight occasions during a year he either fed his Tailor, or, if the Tailor already had eaten elsewhere, gave him some grain and food and liquor to carry home. In contrast Dhem Bahadur, who had just begun to establish himself as an independent householder, only was visited and gave food on two festivals: Dasain and Grandfather-Grandmother. The quality of food and drink also varies. A farmer like Maila Ba, who has plenty or rice, always gives it away on festivals. To maintain status, no matter how poor they may be, all farmers feel they must give rice on at least Tij, Dasain, and Grandfather-Grandmother. But on other festivals there is less stigma attached to giving beer, fried bread, and parched soybeans. At most households where he gets rice, the specialist also expects meat and distilled liquor. The exceptions in Banyan Hill are households that have become Vaishnavite. There has been a notable falling away of festival visits to these farms.

METALWORKERS

Nine of the houses in Metalworker Village provide work on a fairly regular basis to one or more of the Banyan Hill families. Four of the nine belong to ironsmiths; this group, plus the other houses in the settlement whose specialty is iron work, share an open thatched shed where there are forges and anvils. Here they produce sickles, axe heads, spades, cooking utensils, chains, fire tongs, and iron tips for plows. The iron is heated in charcoal that is fanned by hand-operated goatskin bellows. Sometimes when a heavy, thick piece of iron must be shaped, two or three of the men hammer cooperatively, each striking the glowing metal in turn. Another four of the Metalworker houses, which have a regular specialist connection with Banyan Hill, belong to goldsmiths. Goldsmiths generally work separately on the porches of their homes. Their skill is devoted almost entirely to making women's jewelry. They make nose rings, earrings, the small gold flower that women wear in one nostril, necklaces, bracelets, rings, and hair ornaments.

The last of the nine Metalworker houses belongs to a coppersmith, the only one in the community. Much of his work consists of repairing copper water containers, cooking utensils, measures, and lamps; he also makes a few new ones.

All but Uma Maya and Dil Maya have a regular connection with an ironworker family. The most regular kind of work the ironworker is expected to do in return for his payments is sharpening. This work includes putting a good cutting edge on plow tips, axes, mattocks, ditchers, and sickles. The peak load for this kind of work comes before harvests, when all the sickles must be sharpened, and before rice planting when mattocks, ditchers, and plow tips are needed.

Nothing extra is given for sharpening; when the ironworker makes a new implement he often, although not always, is given a rice meal when he brings it to his client. This meal is given in addition to his regular annual payments and is regarded as an optional friendly gesture that will be made when the family can afford it. The iron for new implements is often purchased in Butwal, although the ironworker himself can supply some. Often a farmer will bring two or more old implements and ask the ironworker to use the iron from them to make a single new one.

Payments for the ironworker, with two exceptions, are just like those given the Tailor. In fact, with regard to food on festival occasions, it was sometimes said that the Tailor and the ironworker would be welcome on any occasion when the family had special food, because of all the specialists they were the ones who were just like members of the family. The two exceptions were two extra measures of grain associated with the planting and harvesting of rice. These measures were known as "the ditching implement measure" and "the threshing floor measure." As one might suspect, such payment was made almost without exception only by those who had paddy fields, and reflected the extra work the ironworker had to do for these families as well as their more favorable economic circumstances.

About half of the families in Banyan Hill made regular annual payments to the coppersmith. In return, the smith repaired their copper utensils, such as water vessels, vessels used for cooking the buffaloes' mash, and vessels for making distilled liquor. The annual payment varied. Maila Ba gave the coppersmith about eighteen pounds of paddy each year. Other farmers may give about eight pounds of millet and the same amount of maize. Most give only one eight-pound payment, generally of maize or millet. Those who do make an annual and regular payment consider it cheaper to do this than to pay separately for each repair. The others believe they gain by not making a regular payment. When the smith makes new copper implements for those who pay regularly, he is given a rice meal. If copper is supplied, there is no additional charge for small pieces. For larger pieces, he generally does get a little extra in grain or cash.

Only about one third of the families in the community retain a goldsmith on a regular basis. Again the rationale seems to be a rough comparison of costs, with the choice going to the method that seems cheaper. The goldsmith's work is done on much the same basis as the coppersmith's, and what he receives for it is comparable. Neither the goldsmith nor the coppersmith come to their clients' homes on festival occasions as frequently as the ironworkers and Tailors; whereas Tailors and ironworkers always are given a rice meal if the family has any rice, the coppersmith and goldsmith may be given beer and fried bread.

LEATHERWORKERS

Slightly over half the villagers retain Leatherworkers on a regular basis. The Leatherworkers come from four families: one living in Banyan Hill, two in the adjacent hamlet of Adamara, and one in a more distant Pandera Thum hamlet. In return for their annual payment they supply buffalo gut that is used for fastening the plow to the yoke and for tethering buffaloes in their stalls. Since these thongs last a number of years, there is not a great call for the services of a Leatherworker. They also are expected to remove dead animals; this is a service that Leatherworkers usually will perform whether they are retained or not, since they can sell the hides, and in the case of buffalo, the gut. Families who do not retain a Leatherworker purchase the gut they need for cash. However, Uma Maya, wife of Dubal Singh, paid for two buffalo tethers she needed by carrying manure and wood for a total of four days. The annual payment for the Leatherworker is eight pounds of either millet or maize. In addition, he expects food on a few festivals, such as Dasain and Grandfather-Grandmother. Of all the specialists serving individual families and receiving an annual grain payment, the Leatherworker is fed least frequently on festival occasions.

BRAHMANS

Among the learned Brahmans of Pandera Thum there is a division into *pandit* and *purohit*. A *pandit* is a man who knows Sanskrit well and can conduct lengthy and complicated ceremonies, such as the seven-day-long Saptaha ceremony. Often such a man is referred to as a "great (*thulo*) *pandit*." The *purohit* also knows Sanskrit, but his knowledge is much more limited. He conducts ceremonies; they are, however, the shorter ceremonies such as the Satya Narayan and such domestic ceremonies as those of naming, marriage, and death.

Each of the Banyan Hill Magar families, except for the Headman's plowman, Om Bahadur, is served by a Brahman. In all there are seven Brahmans, and they come from four nearby Brahman hamlets. To the Magar families they regularly serve these men are known as *upret*. They refer to their clients as *jajman*. The *upret* will expect to be called for a Satya Narayan and for naming and other domestic ceremonies. Should the family decide to have a larger ceremony, they would call a *pandit*, but their *upret* would be asked to come and assist. In the more elaborate funeral ceremonies both a *pandit* and the *upret* may be asked to participate.

During the course of the year, there are a number of calendrical festivals on which the *upret* is expected to pay a visit to his *jajman* families. In the month of Srawan (July–August) the World Snake is worshipped on Snake Fifth. This worship of the Snake, sometimes called the Bed of Vishnu and the Garland of Shiva, is carried out first by the head of the house at the spring. In the early morning of November 4, 1961, Dev Bahadur went to his spring, did a godling-type puja there at a small rock shrine, and sacrificed a chicken. Later in the day his *upret* came to his house with a picture he had drawn of four intertwined snakes. The Brahman did puja to the symbol of the World Snake and then pasted it above Dev's door. It would remain there throughout the year, guarding the entrance to the house. Dev then gave the Brahman one pound of rice, a dab of butter, a little salt, a handful of pulse, some tumeric, some cumin seed, and a red pepper. He also gave him half a rupee.

The Brahman who is *upret* to most of the houses in Chepte does not know how to draw the picture of the World Snake. But he comes anyway on this festival and goes from house to house so that his *jajman* will be able to acquire merit by giving him a gift on this auspicious day. Most houses give him a half rupee. Since he does not make the drawing or do a puja, the gift of food is omitted.

In Asoj (September–October) on Tikka Day during the festival of Dasain, the *uprets* again come to visit their families. With them they carry rice, curd, and red coloring materials for tikka. While chanting a verse in Sanskrit, each *upret* gives tikka to all member of his *jajman* family. For his wealthier clients, he brings a little fried sweet bread, but to most he comes empty-handed except for tikka materials. When Jag Maya's *upret* came to her house, she gave him rice, pulse, butter and spices, plus half a rupee. She also gave him a tikka in return for his and some barley sprouts to wear behind his ear.

Brahmans do not visit everyone of their clients on Snake Fifth or even on Tikka Day. There is one occasion when they do visit every house, if at all possible; this is on the festival of Thread Full Moon, a full-moon day that fell in Bhado (August–September) in 1961. On this day the *upret* comes and ties yellow and red yarn around the right wrists of the men and the left wrists of the women. Prior to his visit, he does puja to the Seven Wise Men, legendary seers who are thought to have been translated to heaven and to have become part of the Hindu pantheon. By means of the puja, the colored yarn is sanctified and can carry the blessing of the Wise Men to whomever wears it. The people believe that if they die within six months of putting on the thread, they will go directly to heaven and will avoid purgatory. While tying the threads, the Brahman says a verse in Sanskrit. When he has finished, the person who receives the thread gives him tikka and the usual gift of food and money. The threads are worn until they fall off or until the festival on the following year.

There were only a few other ceremonial occasions besides offerings to the *pitri* for which the *upret* was called during 1960–1961. Two families had marriages elaborate enough to require the services of a Brahman, and two families called their *upret* for naming ceremonies. Four families gave Satya Narayan ceremonies, and Uma Maya gave a ceremony to prevent an inauspicious disposition of the planets from harming her baby son. On each of these occasions, the *upret* received money, rice, and clarified butter.

The Headman's *upret* is much more of a full-time retainer than any of the other *uprets*. He and his wife live most of the time in the Headman's household, and the *upret* helps the Headman conduct his two daily pujas. A major part of the payment that the *upret* receives for his work is in the form of the right to use a large plot of unirrigated land. Since he has a large farm of his own and is a comparatively wealthy man, he estimates that what he receives from the Headman—counting the income from the land, plus what he receives daily as part of the two pujas, and what he receives from the Headman's younger brother, whom he also serves—accounts for only about one third of his yearly income.

MESSENGERS AND FERRYMEN

Moving now from specialists who have occupations associated with their caste and who serve individual Banyan Hill families, we turn to specialists with caste-determined occupations who regularly serve the community as a whole, although they receive their payments from individual families. The three thum messengers may be considered in this category because they always are Untouchables and are paid almost as if they were family retainers. In this category we also may include the members of the Ferryman caste who come regularly to Banyan Hill.

For the support of the three thum messengers, the thum as a whole has been divided into three parts, one part for each. The messenger Banyan Hill supports is a Metalworker who lives in the adjacent Metalworker hamlet. On festival occasions, he visits homes in his constituency to get food and liquor with about the same frequency as the coppersmith. Once a year he also goes about collecting an eight-pound grain payment from each household. On these grain-collecting trips, he often receives liquor; sometimes one meets him dancing down the path, or sitting beside it, waiting for it to become more navigable.

Once a year representatives from the village of Ferrymen on the Kali Gandaki at Kalipar come to Banyan Hill. They go to every house and ask for eight pounds of grain. Only those houses give who have used or expect to use the ferry, but this is most of the houses in the village. The Ferrymen do not collect a fare from people who have given grain. Villagers say the Ferrymen always can remember who has and who has not given.

Caste Distinctness

We have been looking at occupational specialization as a means by which the caste system links groups in a community and brings them together in mutual dependency. But we can look at occupational specialization from a different point of view. Seen in this different way it becomes merely one of a number of attributes that set Pandera Thum caste groups apart from one another. To bring out more of these attributes, we will compare the Magars and other groups, particularly the Brahmans, who are their most numerous neighbors.

As one might expect, there are a number of differences in religious practices between Brahmans and Magars. A Brahman boy wears a string over his right shoulder and under his left arm. This string, or sacred thread, is a status marker and is first put on in an initiation ceremony when the boy is in his early teens. Thus the Brahman not only is set apart from the Magar by the thread, but also by having an additional life-cycle ceremony. In most respects, an elaborate Magar marriage ceremony and the usual Brahman ceremony are similar, but there are some differences in the details. Among the differences is the fact that the bride's people are not invited to the groom's house for a feast, as is the case among the Magars, nor is live sacrifice part of the ceremony. All Brahman families honor their forebears with the same three *sraddha* ceremonies that the Headman's brothers perform. Among the Magars of Banyan Hill and elsewhere this is rare. Brahmans also must do the Satya Narayan ceremony at least once a year, whereas it is optional for Magars. In Pandera Thum, many Brahman families have done the seven-day-long Saptaha ceremony, but only two Magar families have done it. Magars do not work their bulls on the new moon and full moon days nor on one Friday every month, the day when an offering is made to Mandale to prevent attacks by tigers. The Brahmans do not observe this taboo. Brahmans themselves, for religious reasons, do not plow at all. The work is done by hired plowmen. We have noted that although Brahmans worship many of the godlings whom Magars do, such as Hunter Godling, *mari,* and others, in their pujas they include Sanskrit verses from one of the Vedas and never offer live sacrifices. Among differences in the Household Godling puja is the fact that among the Magars the wife helps the husband perform it, while Brahman women are not allowed to see it. Before a Brahman eats, he always offers a little cooked rice to the cooking fire, a practice Magars, as a rule, do not follow. In this connection, it is significant that no Brahman family in Pandera Thum is without at least some irrigated paddy land; there are many Magar families that have none. Rice, the most valued grain, is more closely associated with the Brahman way of life than it is with the Magar way.

Brahmans and Magars seldom sing and dance together, as Brahman tunes differ from Magar tunes. The words of Brahman songs are religious, and are used during ceremonies such as Satya Narayan when Brahman girls dance to them. Magar girls occasionally may dance to these songs with Brahman girls, but the latter seldom are allowed to participate with Magar girls in their singing groups. When an occasional Brahman boy or girl participates in Magar singing groups, this is regarded as somewhat deviant behavior.

Brahman kinship terminology differs from the Magar in ways that reflect the fact that Brahmans forbid marriage with the mother's brother's daughter, and Magars encourage it. Brahman behavior toward kinsmen also varies at a number of points. Behavior such as a Magar's joking with his own or a classificatory mother's brother's daughter is forbidden by the Brahmans, who forbid such joking between any male and female. Brahmans do not have the pattern of marriage by capture, and Brahman women seldom run away from their husbands. If they do, the husband does not collect any compensation.

The Brahman homestead generally looks different than the Magar. Brahmans always have a small earth pedestal within their courtyards, in which is planted the tulsi bush, which is sacred to Vishnu. One rarely finds this in Magar courtyards. Slightly more than half of the Pandera Thum Brahmans are meat eaters, but almost all Magars are. Magars eat chicken and pork, but these meats are taboo for Brahmans, and hence there are no chicken coops or pigpens on Brahman farmsteads. Nor are there stills, for liquor also is taboo for them. Inside the main room of a Magar house there always is a firepit, and cooking is done on a tripod resting in the pit. Brahman houses have no firepit, and cooking is done on a fireplace made of mud and built against a wall.

Until recently most Brahmans knew Sanskrit, being educated either at home or in the thum *pathshala,* a school where the major subject is Sanskrit. Magars were not permitted to study in the thum *pathshala* until recently. Brahmans, on the other hand, were not welcomed in the recruiting depots, and only Magars, a few Thakuris, and Untouchables returned to the thum as pensioned soldiers. These differences colored the stereotypes that each group fostered about the other. The Magar was loyal, generous, and brave but hard drinking and stupid; the Brahman learned but avaricious and cowardly. Physically, Brahmans differ from Magars because they are Caucasoid. In a story that relates one of their physical characteristics to their purported greed, the Magars say that when God was distributing animals among the different castes, he offered the Brahman a choice between a cow and a dog. The Brahman, thinking he could get more milk from a dog because it has more teats, chose it. The long, thin Brahman nose comes from holding it continually due to the smell of the dog's excrement.

The cultural badge of caste distinctness extends to clothing. Brahman girls and women typically wear red turbans and reddish skirts. They also wear a red and gold paper tikkas that they paste to their foreheads. Magar girls and women generally wear white turbans, never red; they buy a different colored skirt material than the Brahmans and wear a different kind of tikka. Sometimes Brahman women use a basket and a tumpline, but it is much more common for them to balance their loads on top of their heads. With the exception of the sacred thread, clothing differences were not as noticeable among the men.

Differences between Magars and Untouchables were also numerous. Among those that played the largest part in giving these groups distinctness was the general Untouchable custom of eating buffalo and the Leatherworkers' custom of eating beef, so long as the animal died a natural death. Untouchables, like the Brahmans, forbade cross-cousin marriage and showed the corresponding differences in their kinship terminology.

Caste Ranking and the Etiquette of Pollution

One basic type of relationship among the caste groups is economic and involves exchanges of skills and food between specialist families and their Magar retainers. Another basic type is one that rests upon the idea of pollution. When looking at intercaste relations from this point of view, one may begin by ordering the caste groups of Pandera Thum according to their ability to pollute other castes, and then one may note a number of ways in which this difference is given expression.

There are thirteen different caste groups in Pandera Thum. With regard to their ability to pollute one another, there is a major cleavage between those groups that are called Touchable (*chhune*) and those called Untouchable (*nachhune*). In addition, there are distinctions within each group, and this distinction also rests on the ability to pollute but does not involve pollution merely by touching one another. This secondary distinction often is spoken of using the term "great" or "big." Thus a Magar belongs to the Touchable group, and this means that he can not pollute any other person merely by touching him with his hand. But within the Touchable group of which he is a member, there are finer distinctions involving ability to pollute, not by touching with the hand, but in other ways such as by touching certain types of cooked food making it inedible. Boiled rice has special importance in this respect, and if a Magar cannot cook rice on his fire and offer it to another man, such as a Brahman, that man's caste is said to be "bigger" or "greater" than his. In Pandera Thum when one asks which group is "biggest" and which "next biggest" and so on, one finds much agreement on the following order among the major groups in the Touchable category:

>Upadhyaya Brahman
>Jaisi Brahman
>Magar-Gurung
>Gharti-Khawase

And for Untouchable caste groups there is much agreement on this order:

>Kami (Metalworker)
>Sarki (Leatherworker)
>Damai (Tailor)

In what follows, we will refer to this ordering as the caste hierarchy and will speak of one group being "higher" or "lower" in it than another. What will concern us will be some of the ways relative rank in this hierarchy is expressed, with the focus upon the Magars and on illustrative relations among them and some of the other caste groups.

Magar rank in the caste hierarchy relative to Upadhyaya Brahmans is shown in gestures of respect. When a Magar man meets a Upadhyaya Brahman, the Brahman raises his foot and the Magar touches his forehead to it. If the Brahman is young and is meeting an older Magar who is much respected, he will first incline his head and then lift his foot to be touched. Some of the younger educated Magar boys do not follow the pattern. When the educated son of the Headman meets a Upadhyaya Brahman, he does not make any gesture of respect, unless his father is present. In this situation, he simply inclines his head and the Brahman touches him on the forehead with his hand.

Magars also show respect for Upadhyaya Brahmans by addressing the men as "grandfather" and the women as "grandmother"; a Magar woman who visits a Upadhyaya Brahman home where the verandah has been freshly cleaned touches her forehead to one of the steps.

The Magar position in the caste hierarchy relative to a Touchable group such as the Ex-Slaves is expressed in similar behavior, although there is more effect here of community standing based on wealth and power than in the case of the Upadhyaya Brahmans. All Magars are likely to show gestures of respect to all Upadhyaya Brahmans, whereas Ex-Slaves are likely to reserve comparable behavior for the wealthier Magar families. An Ex-Slave man, for example, touches his forehead to the foot of the Headman's son; the woman Ex-Slave, neighbor of Maila Ba, touches her forehead to Maila Ba's freshly cleaned verandah step.

Customs regarding food and water are very sensitive indicators of relative position in the caste hierarchy. As foods become more and more "critical," or subject to pollution, the Magars can accept them from fewer and fewer caste groups. Foods that are not subject to ritual pollution include oranges, mangoes, and uncooked grain. Magars can accept these from all other castes. As soon as foods are cooked they become somewhat more critical. Nothing that Untouchables cook can be eaten by Magars, and some very meticulous Magars will not accept ripe fruit from Untouchables. If food is cooked in butter, a substance that may not always come from the sacred cow but that is associated with that animal, even when made of buffalo milk, Magars can accept it from any member of the Touchable group. Boiled rice is a most critical food. If the rice is boiled in "pure" water, Magars can accept it from the kitchens and eat it on the utensils of any caste higher than they in the caste hierarchy. But if it is boiled in water that is not pure—in the sense that some of it has been poured from the container in which it was drawn and used for some purpose other than cooking—then only the Upadhyaya Brahman can serve it to Magars. This group also is the only one from whom the Magars will accept ground cooked millet and cooked black pulse.

If a cooking or eating utensil is made of clay, it can be polluted at any time by the touch of an Untouchable. Only when they are wet can metal or lead utensils be polluted. To remove pollution from a wet utensil, one can fill it with water and hold it over a fire; one can put live coals in it and pour water over them; or one can let it dry in the sun. To remove pollution due to touch, one asks any member of a Touchable caste group to sprinkle one with a little water.

Marriage, of course, is a very sensitive area of relationship between castes. In India the general rule is strict caste endogamy, but in Nepal this rule has been considerably relaxed within the two large "compartments," Touchability and Untouchability. In Pandera Thum, it is very rare for Touchable women to marry Touchable men belonging to castes lower in the hierarchy than their own, but it does occur; when it does, they fall to the status of their husband.

In Banyan Hill, the Ex-Slave living with Indra Kumari married a Magar woman. In caste status she became an Ex-Slave; any children would also have been Ex-Slaves. One of Om Bahadur's wives had been an Ex-Slave, and for all ritual and social purposes his two daughters by her were regarded as Ex-Slaves, although some claimed they belonged to a separate caste called *Khawase*. When a Magar man marries a woman lower then he in rank, such as an Ex-Slave, he can retain his Magar status so long as he does not take foods from his wife that she could pollute. If she were an Ex-Slave, he would have to cook his own boiled rice on a separate fire.

We have been speaking of quite obvious expressions of difference in caste status. Some expressions are much more subtle. An instance of this kind of expression was seen when a Magar and a Brahman were dickering over the sale of a buffalo. It was not that the Magar could not stand up to the Brahman. It was the tinge of arrogance in the Brahman's manner and his rather highhanded way of dealing, both of which were more typical than idiosyncratic. The Brahman and his brother-in-law had come and looked the buffalo over. The Magar had asked Rs 400, and the Brahman had offered Rs 340. The Magar's wife came down to Rs 380. The Magar finally said he would sell it to any man who would give him Rs 360. The next day the Brahman had returned with an offer of Rs 350, and soon afterwards men from a distant village had come and offered Rs 360. At this the Brahman said he also would pay Rs 360, to which the other group replied with an offer of Rs 380. At this point the Brahman spoke in a very magisterial way to the Magar, reminding him that he had been willing to sell for Rs 360 and pointing out to him that he had duties as a neighbor and should send the other bidders away. The Magar agreed, but as soon as they had left the Brahman said he would pay only Rs 350. When the Magar refused, the Brahman and his brother-in-law stalked off behind the cattle shed. When they came back the Brahman called out, "Lo, Kanchhu! Here is the price of the buffalo: Rs 350." The Magar again refused, and they turned angrily away and went back behind the shed.

"The greedy man is weeping," commented the Magar.

Finally, after much more argument and a number of returns to the buffalo shed, the Brahman threw out another five rupee note, and the Magar went and untied the buffalo and helped him lead it away.

8

Work, Song and Dance Groups

Work Groups

THE MOST COMMON kind of work group is formed on the basis of what is called *porima,* or *orima porima,* which means lending an arm, or in our idiom, lending a hand. This kind of exchange is especially suited to a family such as Lakshmi Devi's, which is too poor to hire labor. The family, however, has a number of able young men and boys who can acquire the labor needed for peak seasons on their farm by making work exchanges. Sociability is a factor, but the system rests on the fact that different fields are ready for different processes (planting, weeding, hilling, harvesting) at different times. What needs to be done must be done rapidly, and this requires more labor than the family alone can provide. In order to weed Lakshmi Devi's millet, it took a total of eighteen days of work, not counting her labor and her sons.' There were twelve people from Chepte involved, and some worked for more than a day. The work day began following the main mid-morning meal and continued until late afternoon. During the afternoon, all workers were fed *orni,* or tiffin. This consisted of plates of parched field corn, pickled cucumber, and beer. In return for this assistance, Lakshmi Devi and her sons returned a day or two of work to the family of each member of the group. Usually such returns are made by doing the same kind of work, but this is a tendency only. They could as well make the return by hilling or harvesting maize. Whatever the nature of the work, the return generally is made within a year. If help has not been asked for and given by then, the obligation usually lapses. Labor debts of this kind seldom went unpaid. Families gave help because they had needs of their own.

Groups also are formed on the basis of wage payments. Such groups often are found working for families such as Havildar Santa Prasad's, which have almost no extra labor but a fairly good cash income, whether as a result of a pension or because of a large productive farm. In order to weed his millet, an operation that requires someone to make a hole with a mattock and someone else to set the plant, the Havildar hired a group of twenty Magars, Metalworkers, and Leatherworkers who worked a total of forty-three days. Some worked for only one day and others worked for four. They all were given *orni* and were paid in pig meat at a rate of a pound of meat for a day's work. Santa Prasad had to hire labor because his wife only recently had had a baby and there was no way he could repay labor obtained on an exchange basis. Hiring labor for wages as he had to do is called *nemiki* (wages).

A third kind of group appears on farms whose owners are poor and at the same time have little labor for setting up exchanges. Om Bahadur did not have bulls of his own; the Headman's bulls, which he normally would have used for planting his maize, had been much pulled down by working the Headman's land. To help him out, his brother-in-law from a nearby hamlet came with his bulls and plowed for four days. This was understood as "help within the family," which is called *madat;* the only return expected is a good rice meal, if possible with meat and liquor, and an *orni*. Another person who benefitted much from *madat* was Uma Maya, whose four married daughters used to come with their husbands. She had no bulls of her own, and her sons-in-law did much of her plowing for her and also helped with other kinds of fieldwork.

A fourth kind of group is almost exclusively associated with the task of carrying wood from the forest to the farm. As noted above, Magars do not use their bulls on new moon days, full moon days, and on one Friday a month, when puja to Mandale is done. All three of these days have special religious significance and are days when good deeds acquire added merit. If a man has cut and stacked wood and needs a dozen people or so to carry it to his farmstead, he will go around to his neighbors' houses on one of these days, or beforehand, and ask for help. This kind of help is referred to not as *madat,* but as *saghau*. Magars feel that one should not work on the full moon, new moon, and Mandale puja days. Work that is called *saghua* does not fall under the ban, nor does fishing, a common group activity on such days, even though the arduous method employed requires diversion of a stream from its original bed. When *saghau* is provided, the workers expect to receive *orni,* but they do not expect a specific return. The work is done out of neighborliness and for the sake of their own souls. For carrying his wood, Bir Bahadur obtained help from twenty people on *saghau*. The use of *saghau* groups is not limited to any type of farm. The Headman and his brothers, as well as a very poor farmer like Bir Bahadur, depend upon them.

Groups formed on the basis of *saghau* always consist of people who are there on no other basis. This also is strictly true of groups that come on a *madat* basis to thatch houses. Those who come usually are relatives and they expect no more than a rice meal and an *orni*. There is no expressed reason. It is merely felt to be wrong to thatch a house roof on any other basis. This is true even when relatives do not do the work. A Leatherworker helped thatch Uma Maya's house and the work was considered *madat*. When he thatched her verandah and cowshed, however, he worked on a *porima* basis, and she owed him two days of return labor. It is doubtful if a relative would have made this distinction between house and outbuildings, because the general rule is that *any* roofing should be done as *madat*. Groups that work on other processes, such as planting, weeding, and harvesting, can be and often are mixed. A mixture of *porima* and *nemiki* is especially common.

PAYMENTS

Wages are paid in either cash or kind; although there is fluctuation with demand, they vary around a commonly accepted standard of equivalents. People who work for the wealthier farmers frequently want butter, and many take butter on account prior to doing the work. A day's work is worth a quarter of a pound of butter; this in turn is roughly equivalent to the same amount of mustard oil, one-half pound of kerosene oil, a pound of salt, eight pounds of millet, or one rupee. When labor is not in great demand it is possible to get a day's work for half a rupee, but it would be more difficult to reduce the amount paid in kind by that much. Rice threshing, even when it is not regarded as *madat,* frequently is paid for as if it were. Depending on the length of time worked, people get either one rice meal and an *orni* or two rice meals and an *orni*. However, the workers realize they could ask for an equivalent amount of uncooked rice, but this is something relatives who came to work on *madat* would not be likely to do.

Bulls and a plowman are paid for by counting them as twice what a man alone is worth. A team of bulls and a man working for one day are repaid by two days of work on a *porima* basis. Here, too, of course, there is fluctuation due to demand. Bulls and a plowman sometimes cost as much as three rupees per day, where the usual price would be only two. Occasionally labor is paid for by giving the worker a wicker basket. During the rainy season, a popular payment is a local umbrella made of two layers of thinly woven wickerwork with large leaves laid in between.

COMPOSITION

Any work group tends to be composed of a nucleus of persons, especially young people, who almost always work together. Dhem Bahadur of Chepte and Tara Maya's son were the center of a group of boys and girls from that side of the hamlet. The Adamara headman's daughters usually worked with a Leatherworker girl from their hamlet and with Ganga, who stayed with Sita Devi of Darkang. As groups enlarge, nuclei such as these are increased and the additions are quite predictable. The adult men and women of Chepte, plus Dirgha Singh and his wife and Bir Bahadur and his wife, along with Metalworkers from Metalworker Village and some Ex-Slaves from another adjacent hamlet very frequently worked together. As the Darkang group expanded, it included the adults of the lineage plus Magars and Leatherworkers from Adamara and a few Brahman young people who lived nearby. It can be seen that work groups create interlacings between the people in single sections of Banyan Hill and the hamlets adjacent to them. Yet the groups also make connections within Banyan Hill itself from one neighborhood to another. Kanchha Ba's sons or Saila Ba's daughter-in-law joined groups in Darkang as well as in Chepte, and Dirgha Singh and his bulls frequently were seen in Darkang.

The only kind of work group that did not have this quality of expansion around fairly permanent nuclei was a group known as *pehari*. The young people in Banyan Hill did not form such a group, but one did come to work there. This group was composed of fourteen people, most of them in their late teens and early twenties. They hired themselves out as a group, working for a rupee a day. They saved the money they earned, and at the end of a season would use it to purchase a feast. A key figure in the group, and one of the two middle-aged persons, was a Gurung woman of about fifty who was a fine singer—"like a girl fifteen or sixteen." People were attracted to the group because they enjoyed field labor when she was leading the songs.

The usual work group not only cut across neighborhood lines but also differences in age. Participants ranged from late childhood to old age. With the exception of some kinds of work such as paddy and millet planting, where women did one task and men another, or house roofing, which was reserved for men alone (though women could hand up the straw), members of a work group all engaged in the same tasks; all sang the same songs and enjoyed the same jokes. The groups also cut through caste lines, including the complete range from Untouchable to Brahman; they also tended to level distinctions of wealth. In *porima*, especially, there were young people from all families regardless of their economic condition. A group carrying wood on *saghau* included Maila Ba's wives, and family members from the poorest of Chepte Metalworker Village and Ex-Slave houses. The only basis for forming work groups that excluded the wealthier families was *nemiki*. There was some feeling that working for wages carried a slight stigma. But as *porima* workers, members of these families frequently worked side by side with people who were on a *nemiki* basis.

Interpersonal relations in Banyan Hill are pulled in a nonegalitarian direction by the caste system and by large differences in wealth. There are, however, strong forces working in a counter-direction. Among the strongest of these forces are the song and dance groups; especially important are the many days of companionship and sociability that most people, in their youth if not when older, have spent working together.

Song and Dance Groups

Many Magar songs are associated with the fieldwork of particular seasons. There are songs sung while millet is being planted and others that accompany the rice planting. The songs, with lines that are sung by men and women alternately, make this difficult, stooping work go more easily. Other occasions have their characteristic songs also. One type of song is sung by boys and girls as they walk together along the paths on the way to a songfest or singing contest. There are songs sung by women Ex-Slaves on various occasions during a marriage; others are sung only by women during the days between Krishna's birthday in Bhado (August–September) and the following festival of Tij. Women also dance to these songs; there are special songs for the day during Tivahar when offerings are made to Lakshmi, goddess of wealth, and songs for Brother-Worship Day.

RODI

On many occasions during the year, but especially during festival seasons such as Dasain, groups of boys and girls called *rodi* gather together on some centrally located trailside sitting place such as the one in the Deorali bazaar. The groups usually consist of young people from a number of nearby villages and may include persons from the Tailor, Metalworker, and Leatherworker castes, as well as Magars, who generally predominate. Occasionally a Brahman boy joins and more rarely a Brahman girl. Some of the boys have drums. Many also have flashlights and there is much shining of lights into the faces of girls and new arrivals. The gatherings consist of from twenty to thirty young people.

There are characteristic tunes and a characteristic method of singing. About half a dozen tunes are sung commonly, and they vary in speed. The basic pattern of the singing is question and answer. The boys in the group will make one of their number the song leader. He will select any one of the tunes and will sing a question. The whole group then repeats the question in song, often three times. One of the girls informally chosen as leader sings an answer, which the group repeats. This goes on indefinitely. When the group is tired of one tune, someone will suggest a change. A change in tunes, however, brings little change in the basic pattern of boy-girl question and answer. The subject matter seldom varies: all the questions and answers have to do with love, marriage, and a bantering sexual antagonism between the boys and girls.

There is variation in details of the way words are used in the various tunes. Generally there are two lines in each question and answer. In some tunes, the first line of a verse is invariably the same. Only the question varies, and if possible it will be made to rhyme with the first line. In other songs both lines can vary.

Such singing would seem to place great emphasis on the ingenuity of the song leaders. While it is true that they must be quick witted, with much of the fun depending upon how they can seize on the developing situation, it is not quite as difficult as it may seem; even where both lines are free, the first line need not have any meaningful relation to the second, which contains the question. Also, there are a great many stock first lines as well as stock question and answer lines to go with them. Good song leaders have a large repertoire of these standardized lines; if their invention flags, others in the group can take their place and help them out. The following lines, similar to those inserted in a tune called *Lalu-mai*, will provide an example of free but standardized first lines and the kind of question and answer that can go with them:

Boy song leader: How beautifully the kite flies in the sky.
　　　　　　　　When did we first love one another, you and I?

These verses are repeated twice by the whole group.

> Girl song leader: Rice grows near the village, where the goats used to graze.
> We first began to love when we were weeding maize.

These verses are repeated twice by the whole group.

In a tune called *Niri Maya* the first standardized line always is: "Don't you know, Eldest daughter Niri Maya, that I am yours?" The song leaders then sing the question or the answer. There are tunes, although rarely sung, in which the boys sing generally standardized verses and the girls join in a chorus. These are not nearly as interesting to the participants.

As the evening wears on, there is more and more intermingling of boys and girls, whose groups initially were separate. A girl who is fond of a boy will lie with her head in his lap. Occasionally contact of this kind even occurs across caste lines, with a Magar girl, for example, permitting a Metalworker boy to put his arm around her. (On arriving at home after contact of this kind, the Magar girl of course would ask to be sprinkled with water.) Much courtship occurs during the songfests. The intimacy that group singing provides is very helpful for young people whose marriages are not arranged, for a man who has lost his wife and is seeking another, or for a married man who is seeking a second wife.

In songs of the kind we have been discussing, the focus is upon the two groups of boys and girls. When the leaders need help, or even when someone else merely wants to contribute, persons other than the leaders are free to sing. But there are tunes that are recognized as the vehicle for contests of wits between a single girl and a single boy. These songs sometimes are entered into with the agreement that if the girl loses she must marry the boy. Losing consists of being unable (or perhaps pretending to be unable) to reply to questions that are put or statements that are made. As already noted, the youngest sister of the Banyan Hill headman is said to have "sung dumb" a boy opponent in a contest that lasted for three nights.

When a man, who now is middle-aged, was a youth, there used to be special huts called *rodighar* where the young people would gather and sing. These huts were used during the winter months; during the warmer weather trailside resting places would be used, as they are now. This man remembered three such huts in the immediate vicinity of Banyan Hill. The usual custom was for girls of the locality to invite the boys to come and sing. The girls would provide liquor and food, and the boys would help defray expenses by bringing money.

In the *rodighar,* a hukka was part of the courtship pattern and was shared by boys and girls. Today its role has been superseded by cigarettes. When a boy offers a packet of cigarettes and a matchbox to a girl, he holds one hand beneath the other in an elaborate gesture of respect. She may reply, "Why should I accept your cigarettes? We are poor in my village. I accept them from you tonight and enjoy them. But who will supply me tomorrow when you are gone?" And the boy answers, "Mother's Brother's Daughter, you are making me uncomfortable. You're really saying I'm so poor I'll miss this packet of cigarettes." Banter in this vein goes on a long time before a girl accepts a packet.

KAHAURA

During the nights, from Holy Fifth (January 21 in 1961) and lasting until the second day of the Dasain festival, one is likely to hear a particular song tune accompanied by many drums beaten in unison. The drumming and chorusing of boys and girls often only gives way at dawn to the thump-pound of the rice-huller or the Brahman's taut up-gliding note on a conch shell. If one goes to investigate, one finds a group of Magar girls and young men, with an occasional older married man, in one of the thum courtyards. The young men sit in a row on the ground and beat small circular drums, open on one end. They use one hand to strike the drum and it gives a flat, nonresonant note unlike the deeper, mellower tone of the various two-headed drums. The boys sing loudly as they play and take their words and cues from one of the number who acts as song leader. While they are singing and beating the drums, unmarried girls varying in number from one to about seven and wearing shawls over their heads, gyrate slowly about in front of the boys, dancing in time to the music. The end of a song is announced by a special rhythmic pattern on the drums, and when this appears the dancers begin to lower themselves to the ground so that at the end of the song they squat facing the boys with their shawls held before their faces. The same dance pattern is repeated over and over again throughout the night. Only the words of the songs vary. Some of the young men present do not have drums, and they sit behind the drummers. Occasionally one of them gets up and waves a rupee note or a cigarette in front of the girls. They pretend not to notice but suddenly will snatch for the object, while the man tries to pull it away before they can get it. The young people, who always are Magars, come together throughout a season and are known as a *kahaura* group. The young men and girls together provide the food and liquor that is consumed during the course of the evening.

JHABRE

Another type of song and dance, not exclusively Magar, is called the *jhabre*. One occasion on which it occurred was the eighth evening of Dasain, at the thum's ritual centre which is located on the height of the ridge behind Banyan Hill. Young people began to gather while a Brahman was performing a ceremony in the kot temple. Following this ceremony, at moondown, the young people formed four ragged groups. Each consisted of both boys and girls, and there were some older people who sat around as spectators. When the moon set, it became very dark. There was one lantern; two Magar brothers, both a little drunk and leaning on one another, carried it unsteadily from group to group.

Each group gradually formed a rough circle, with boys and girls leaning against one another side by side. Boys who came late and could not enter stood on the outside and leaned backwards against a girl.

The *jhabre* song began slowly and then speeded up. At the conclusion of each stanza, when the rhythm was most rapid, the men gave a series of high-pitched shouts—"Ha! Ha! Ha! Ha!" Until it became monotonous through repetition, the effect was headily exciting. Inside each circle, one of the boys did a solo dance until he was tired and relieved by another. One of the indefatigable dancers was an older married man, an ex-soldier, who wore an army beret with insignia and khaki shorts. Following the usual pattern, at the beginning of each stanza of the song he jerked his hips and then started rotating slowly, pushing one foot ahead of the other. As the rhythm became more rapid, he would twirl more and more rapidly, lowering himself closer and closer to the ground and waving his arms about over his head. Then as the stanza drew to a close and the men shouted, he would leap into the air again and again as high as he could.

The crowd consisted of Magars and the three Untouchable castes, Metalworkers, Tailors, and Leatherworkers. Two of the goldsmith Metalworkers had just returned from India where they had found employment. Both wore short mountain skirts and were barefooted; as evidence of their recent journey, they wore dark glasses and sweaters, with new wrist watches strapped outside the sweaters.

As the evening wore on it got very cold, and the dew was heavy. A few of the girls had umbrellas and opened them to keep the dew off. Some of the boys who had drunk a lot went to one side, lay down in the wet grass, and went to sleep. But most of the crowd remained on their feet, singing or dancing until the sky in the east began to grow light.

NACHARI

Besides secular singing groups such as these, there are three exclusively Magar, all-male religious singing groups in Pandera Thum. Their songs and dancing are spoken of as *nachari*.

On November 9, 1961, the dark night of the moon (*aunsi*) during Tivahar, a *nachari* group was invited to the Adamara headman's courtyard. Guests from the neighborhood, wrapped in shawls, crowded together on his verandah. The group, which sang about the life of Lord Krishna, consisted of four dancers, four drummers, and a cymbal player. There also were a number of singers. The dancing and singing began past midnight and continued with short breaks until mid-morning. The dancers were young boys, and they danced in a series of slow simple patterns in front of the mostly middle-aged instrumentalists and singers. Two of the dancers were dressed like girls, with velvet blouses, necklaces, bracelets, and pigtails. They represented the milkmaids whom Lord Krishna loved. The other two dancers were dressed to represent Lord Krishna and his brother, Balarama. They wore crowns of paper and tinsel, yellow tunics, and pleated white skirts. All four moved their hands and arms with fluid grace as they kept time to the drums. At the end of each section, like the girls in the *kahaura* dance, they squatted down on the ground.

The dance had opened with the drummers and the cymbalist playing alone without any singing; after this introduction, one of the singers had thrown rice and water over the four dancers to purify them so that they would be ready to simulate revered gods and goddesses. After this, the singers had joined the drummers in an introductory song. Following another pause when the drumming had begun again, two of the men, one of whom was a drummer, started to shake; soon their whole bodies were caught up in the movement. They had become possessed by the goddess, Saraswati, the patron goddess of *nachari* groups. Their state of trance lasted about three minutes and then left as quickly as it had come. It was auspicious for them to become possessed because it showed the goddess was present and enhanced the religious aura in which *nachari* songs and dances take place. The *nachari* has a very slow rhythm. During the breaks throughout the night to relieve the monotony and revive some of the spectators who had gone to sleep or were dozing, the group sang popular secular songs with a more spritely rhythm.

The *nachari* groups begin their performances on Krishna's birthday, (September 2, 1961). Thereafter, they can sing and dance until some time during the month of Phagun (February–March) when the season is closed by a puja to Saraswati. In 1962, the puja of one of the groups took place on the fourth of March. It is believed that illness and death will result if *nachari* songs or dances are performed during the balance of the year.

The central figure in the *nachari* group is the song leader, called *gur* (for *guru* or teacher). The songs generally are learned by apprenticing oneself to a practicing *gur* and giving a gift, which in one case was a cock and five rupees. The songs consist of excerpts from the *Ramayana* and from the life of Lord Krishna, and the leader sings phrases that are then repeated in chorus by the other singers. A good leader will know enough verses to keep the group performing, with breaks for food, for two days and two nights.

The group closest to Banyan Hill was a group that sang the *Ramayana* and included about thirty-two men and boys. It had been started by the grandfather of the present leader and had had four leaders in all since its inception. Like other groups, it sang on invitation; during the 1961–62 season it had been called on five occasions: to Tara Maya's, when she had a Satya Narayan puja for the welfare of her soldier son; to a nearby Brahman house on the same *aunsi* when the other group performed at the Adamara headman's; to a nearby hamlet as part of the Grandfather-Grandmother festival; and to another hamlet simply for religious entertainment.

A traditional procedure is followed when making payments on these occasions. All of the people who come to the performance bring millet, unhulled rice, or maize. The amounts vary, but most houses bring at least a few pounds. The grain is placed in containers on a large tray supplied by the host family. The host family also supplies a smaller brass tray of hulled rice. Leaves are placed on one side of this smaller tray, and the audience places small amounts of money on them. On the other side of the tray, on a second group of leaves, families who wish may put additional money with which they purchase a share in a feast that will be held at the close of the *nachari* season. *Nachari* groups keep lists of those who have purchased shares, and the money is used for purchasing goats and liquor. The grain that is collected on the larger tray also is saved for the feast.

The host who invites the *nachari* group is expected to provide a heavier grain contribution than the guests, although he need not buy a share. He will be invited to the feast regardless. If he releases the group before the mid-morning meal, it is not necessary for him to do more than give them liquor and fried breads for the early morning meal. But if the performers stay through the day, he must feed them all meals. His guests bring fried breads for the performers and occasionally liquor.

For the closing puja to Saraswati, the dance group builds a stone, tiered shrine, and the clothing of the dancers is bundled up and hung from a pole beside it. Two of the dancers act as *pujaris,* and the major offerings are puffed rice and milk. The puja is carried out to *nachari* music, and during the course of it one or more of the singers or drummers usually becomes possessed.

The group that sang in the Adamara headman's courtyard illustrates one of the ways by which *nachari* songs diffuse. This group was taught their version of the Krishna story by a soldier from their lineage when he came home on leave. He also supplied much of the costuming. During this man's thirty-six years of service, which included Gallipoli in the first World War and Monte Cassino in the Second, he had become much interested in *nachari*. This interest was stimulated by this father, who was himself a *nachari* song leader. He obtained his version of the Krishna story, a version different from his father's, when he was temporarily assigned to a post with a Gurung battalion. Liking their tunes and dances, he joined their *nachari* group and learned their version. He also paid their leader to copy the text for him. When he returned to his own battalion, he taught the Magars there the new version and became their leader. While on leave, he taught the new version to his brother, who is the present leader of the group.

A second kind of religious dance, called *ghanto,* had disappeared in Pandera Thum. To hear and see it one had to go to other thums, where it also appeared to by dying out. It purported to be the story of the *Ramayana,* but the connection was faint. It told the story of a number of queens, all wives of the same king, and how they died and were restored to life again by the *ghanto* songs. The participants are young girls and women, and the two-day dance takes place at the time of the spring full moon in an intensely religious atmosphere, with elaborate and colorful costuming.

9

Politics and Recent Change

The Headman

THE BANYAN HILL headman, focus of political activity in Banyan Hill and the surrounding region, inherited his position from his father, by whose family the office had been held for many generations. But his ascendancy was his own creation, the result of his astuteness and talents.

There are eight headmen in the whole of Pandera Thum. Three are Brahman, and the remainder are Magar. In return for keeping the peace, acting as liaison officers between the government and the people, and collecting taxes—the most important of which is the one on unirrigated farm land—the headmen receive five percent of what they collect. However, since taxes are extremely low, this form of income is not the major reward of office. The real reward lies in the days of forced labor the headmen can claim from each household within their respective jurisdictions. Legally, this custom was abolished following the overturning of the Rana regime; in actual fact it is continuing, at least in the case of the Banyan Hill headman. This is understandable, for it is difficult to enforce laws made in Kathmandu that run contrary to long-established hill practice. A more basic problem also is involved. The headmen are necessary to the government. They perform an essential service not just because they collect taxes, but also because they entertain traveling government officials, secure the necessary labor for carrying out projects such as road repair, provide the government with information on local developments, and settle disputes among villagers that otherwise would crowd the district courts. Their position saddles them with considerable responsibility and it makes demands on their time and resources. The repeal of the law that enabled them to obtain forced labor deprived them of compensation without relieving them of any duties. Their duties in fact tended to increase, because the government had turned its attention to village improvement. They naturally are reluctant to give up their most valuable form of compensation. The government, in turn, realizing their value and the difficulty of enforcing the new regulation, finds it difficult to press the issue. In Banyan Hill the results of forced labor abolition were not uniform. Weaker headmen found it difficult to maintain the pattern. Their constitutents had learned of the law, and they very often felt they could defy the demands of their headmen. But a strong headman, such as the one from Banyan Hill, could continue the custom almost without change. People feared him. People needed him because he was a source of loans in cash or grain. Many of the people recognized that he was a community benefactor. Without him, community life would have run less smoothly. If forced labor was an injustice, it was believed by many to be a lesser injustice than they might have suffered from other powerful persons in the community. The Banyan Hill headman had a reputation for just dealings, and they could win his allegiance and protection by providing labor when he asked for it.

ARBITRATOR AND BENEFACTOR

Almost every morning while the Banyan Hill headman and his Brahman retainer were doing puja, his courtyard would begin to fill with men and women who had come to him for legal advice or for arbitration of a dispute. When the puja was done and the closing hymn had been sung, the Headman would return to his house. Sometimes he sat on the floor of his second storey balcony and those who wished to see him, provided they were members of a clean caste, climbed up the notched pole ladder and squatted before him. Untouchables consulted him from the courtyard below. At other times he sat in the open-sided *dhansar*. This was not regarded as a home but as a storage shed, and a member of any caste could come and consult him here.

Since he could read and write and had taught himself a great deal about the law, many people came to him simply for advice before entering into any legal arrangements. Others came because of misunderstandings or hard feelings that had arisen among themselves and other people. They hoped the Headman could settle their difficulty locally, since this was better than becoming involved in a lengthy, expensive, and embittering court case.

One morning a large number of persons gathered in the courtyard. They were from another village, and their number included an old lady who was a widow. The difficulty was that she had become too feeble to run her farm and had asked her husband's brother's son to come and run it for her. In return for his agreement to look after her the rest of her life, she had given him her property. At the time, the Headman had drawn up documents that gave the situation legal status. But later the old lady changed her mind. She had a falling out with her nephew and wanted control over the land. She and her advisors and the nephew and his—all of whom had some rights in the land—came to the Headman seeking arbitration. He persuaded them all that the nephew should return the land, but he got them to agree as well that when the old lady died the nephew, in return for the help he had already given her, should have first option to purchase her property. While all watched, he destroyed the papers he had drawn up establishing the original arrangement.

That same morning some men and a widow and her widowed daughter-in-law, also had come to see him. The two widows were living together on the same farmstead but were not getting along well, and they had decided to partition the property. They had come to the Headman for advice about how to do this, and he wrote it all out for them in proper legal form.

Later that week, a Magar woman from a nearby village came and complained that a Brahman had taken legal advantage of her. She was illiterate, and he had incorrectly written a legal agreement between them. The Headman sent her back home again, telling her not to worry and promising that he would come personally and investigate. Similarly, he told a Leatherworker's separated second wife that he would come to her village and investigate her charge that her estranged husband had come to her house and taken some copper utensils that belonged to her. The Headman's promises were not idle. It might be some time before he arrived on his pony, but he would come.

Another case that was presented to the Headman on the same day involved a complication due to loss of a wife. The wife ran away with another man who had paid compensation of Rs 300 to the first husband. But then the wife ran away again, this time taking some gold jewelry which belonged to her second husband. She and her third husband (technically her lover) left the village and could not be found. The robbed husband came to the Headman for help, and he sent a messenger to the village of the third husband and asked all his adult male lineage members to come to see him. When they came, they discussed the matter and he sent them back telling them to return with the wife's parents and her first two husbands, or some responsible person to represent them. It was a large group that came on the day we are speaking of. After a long discussion, in which new developments came to light, the group arrived at a number of decisions. It was agreed that the lineage of the potential third husband should take responsibility for the payment of compensation to the second, and they agreed to give him Rs 200. It turned out that the girl and her potential third husband had left some of the gold jewelry with her parents. The parents confessed to this and were able to return all but three of the pieces. These three had been taken away by the fleeing couple. Under pressure because of their collusion, and knowing that the Headman could take the case to court if he wished, they agreed to pay Rs 300 for the missing pieces. But the Headman suggested, and all agreed, that this money should be returned to the parents if the gold were returned within a year.

On the second day following this case, the Headman and a large gathering of men met together in the shade of the huge banyan tree that grew out of the sitting place at the trail juncture near his house. He had taken with him many hanks of bark that had been stripped from logs brought to his courtyard for use as house beams. He cut the bark into thin strips, rubbed them until they were fibrous, and then twisted them into rope. Soon most of the men present were doing the same thing. There were two problems to be discussed. First to be taken up was the request of the shopkeepers in Deorali. It had been predicted by astrologers that violent earthquakes soon would rack Nepal, and the shopkeepers feared that the trees towering over their shops would fall down and destroy them. They wanted permission to cut them down and had sought to put pressure on the Headman by approaching his sons and getting them to agree that there was a danger—getting the youngest, in fact, to agree that at least all the branches should be cut off. But the Headman was unmoved and was able to dissuade them from cutting either branches or trees by pointing out that the trees had been planted as an expression of religious duty. To destroy them would be sacrilegious.

The second case was one involving Dirgha Singh, of the Headman's own lineage. Dirgha had lived with a widow but had not brought her into his own house. She had had a son by him and he had brought the boy home and had brought him up. His relation with the widow and his recognition of his son gave them *joint* legal right to a share of his property. Had he brought the widow home, recognizing her as a second wife, she and the son *each* would have been entitled to a share. When he was in his teens, the son had gone away and had lived with relatives in a distant village. Now he had returned with supporters to claim a share of Dirgha's property.

"What do you think we should do?" the Headman asked Dirgha.

"I have nothing to say," he replied. "I didn't tell the boy he had to go away. If he wants to stay here with me, I'll keep him. I don't know what the law says I'm supposed to do. I'll do what you say. But I don't think he should sell the land to others if he gets it."

"But you have to give him his share if he wants it," the Headman said. "There will have to be a complete partition."

The Headman outlined the procedure, indicating how the property would have to be divided into six equal shares—one each for the claimant and his mother jointly, for Dirgha himself, his present wife, and each of his three sons by her. Dirgha listened and then raised a point of some importance.

"The debts the boy has will have to be considered too, won't they?"

"This is certain," the Headman answered.

Now the son entered the discussion.

"But I can do as I wish with my share," he commented.

"No, you can't do that," said the Headman. "You can't sell without giving your father a chance to buy."

He then began to calculate the amount of land under cultivation, the uncultivated and forested land, and the livestock. He decided that neither the livestock nor the uncultivated land should be distributed. Dirgha would keep his son's share as compensation for what the son owed him.

The Headman next asked the son whether he wanted to go away again or stay in the village. The son said he wanted to go and would sell the land. The Headman and others said that since he was selling to his father, he should not charge too much. The Headman asked for a figure, but neither side was willing to make a suggestion.

The Headman said, "For the sake of discussion, let's say Rs 100 for the share of rice land and Rs 300 for the share of dry land."

He asked for discussion on this point from the important men present, but no one said anything. He asked again, saying, "Some one ought to make a suggestion."

Finally a Brahman for Dirgha's side said, "It's up to them. It's between the father and his son. But actually I think all the land is only worth Rs 350." This aroused hot discussion between Dirgha and his son. The son and his supporters—two Brahmans who were brothers—argued that all the land was worth at least Rs 370. Finally, after the argument had gone on for some time and had diminished somewhat in intensity, the Headman spoke.

"It's only a question of Rs 20. Let it be decided at Rs 350."

Both sides agreed, and in their agreement on the lower figure one glimpsed the Headman's skill as arbitrator and could understand why hill people say it is good to belong to the village of a strong headman. This is not to imply that injustice was done. Justice, however, can be tempered and all recognized that in this case it was tempered slightly in favor of the father.

When one thinks of the Headman as benefactor of the community, it is impossible to separate the roles of headman and religious man. But one can consider those beneficial aspects of his role that are religiously motivated but are at the same time least closely associated with Brahmans. As such a benefactor perhaps the most important of his accomplishments was a series of channels and small ponds that he had planned for the people of Pandera Thum. The purpose was to bring water to places in the thum that were so far from springs that it was difficult to carry the water needed for livestock. The waterworks were not intended to be a substitute for the springs, which still were to be used for drinking water. They were intended only as a supplement. The channels he got people to build stretched for a number of miles; besides the initial labor of constructing them, labor was required to keep them open. He also saw to this, occasionally doing some of the work himself. But more often he was able to get persons from each locality to do it, and from time to time he hired a man to go over the whole system and make repairs.

His activities as a water engineer were not limited to his own thum. A few miles away there was a hamlet on a hilltop whose water supply was so far distant that it took a number of hours to go to and from the spring. The Headman examined the area and found that by channeling, water could be brought much closer. Since a conservative and influential person in the hamlet was not convinced the idea would work, the Headman was not able to persuade the people of this community to help with the task themselves. But he was able to get people from his own thum to join him. When they had built the project and demonstrated it would work, the people of the skeptical community took it over and maintained it.

The Kot

The kot is a symbol of the political and religious unity of the thum and of the interpenetration of these two spheres. The fortress that used to surmount the hill has disappeared. Only a few low walls remain, plus a tradition that claims that a stone with a groove in it, which rests in the valley below and can be seen from a jutting ledge beside the fortress ruins, was used for target practice by bowmen who stood on the ledge. There are two structures now on the kot hilltop. There is a small shrine for Barahi, consort of Shiva. This stone and wood structure is not enclosed and is maintained and used by the Brahman community of the thum. The other structure is the kot temple. It is made of stone with a thatched roof and is large enought to hold three or four people. A short distance away in front of it, toward the east, the sod has been lifted to make a bare earth circle. In the center of the circle there is a wooden post about five feet high and carved at the top in a simple geometric design. The goddess who resides in the kot temple is Durga, another consort of Shiva, and animals offered to her are sacrificed while tied to the wooden post. Durga is an appropriate goddess for the kot, since she is associated with arms and military might. The kot temple is maintained by the thum as a whole.

SMALL DASAIN: POLITICAL AND RELIGIOUS COMPLEMENTARITY

The two most important ceremonial occasions at the kot are the two Dasain festivals—both the major festival that takes place in the fall and a smaller festival known as Chaitre or Small Dasain that takes place in March—April. Many of the essential elements of kot ceremonial with their symbolic implications can be seen in the Small Dasain ritual, which takes place in a single day as compared to eleven days required for completion of the more elaborate fall ritual. The initial portion emphasizes the importance of the Brahman community. In the spring of 1961, twenty-two Brahman men, women, and children came to the kot on the morning of Small Dasain. Although the major purpose for coming was to allow the men to worship at the Barahi shrine, the spirit was that of a family outing and picnic. The group carried cooking utensils and planned to remain for a meal on the mountain top, having as a main dish the goat that would be sacrificed to the goddess. The people all came from a nearby Brahman hamlet. If they had not been able to come, Brahmans from any other thum hamlet would have taken the responsibility. The aim of worship at the kot was the good health and good fortune of the thum as a whole.

Worship at the Barahi shrine followed the usual Brahman pattern but was augmented on this occasion by reading the whole of a long Sanskrit text. A number of the Brahman men participated, each reading aloud from his own book. The men squatted under a low, open thatched shelter, facing the snowy white Annapurna range that loomed to the north. This part of the ceremonial at the kot was dominated exclusively by Brahmans except at one point. When it came time to offer a small black kid to the goddess, an unmarried Magar boy, the sister's son of the Hill Village headman, performed the sacrifice. In preparation he had bathed in the morning, put on ritually pure clothing, and fasted. (As it happened, the goat actually was beheaded by the boy's father, as the boy was too small to do it at one blow. By touching the blade used by his father, however, it was as if the boy himself had performed the act, and the boy did drag the body of the goat around the shrine.) The sacrifice of the goat penetrated the circle of Brahman dominance in another way, also, since the goat was provided by the thum as a whole through the mediation of the office of headman. Symbolically, the Barahi ceremony stood for the importance of Brahman intercession with divinity for thum welfare. It also symbolized, although this aspect was more muted, the connection between the sacred, as represented by Sanskritic rituals and Brahmans, and the secular, as represented by the goat and its sacrifice. The actual killing of the goat underlined the connection between politics and force of arms.

The second part of the Small Dasain ritual took place at the kot temple and the sacrificial circle. Administratively, the central figure now was the Hill Village headman. His authority in this locality was shown by an incident that occurred later in the year during the major Dasain festival. The Brahman who was performing the rituals at the kot had made preparations to sanctify the buffalo calf that was to be sacrificed at the post in the sacrificial circle. The Brahman asked the unmarried Magar boy who was to behead the calf to come and perform the worship under his direction. When the Hill Village headman saw what the priest had decided to do, he objected by saying that it was a task that the Brahman himself should perform. Without any hesitation, the priest took over from the boy. It is inconceivable that the headman would have assumed similar authority a short distance away at the Barahi shrine. There he stood to one side diffidently and watched the goings-on, for unlike the kot area it was not a place where he was expected to play a guiding role.

In the Small Dasain ritual, the headman had arranged to have one of the Brahmans in the group at the Barahi shrine come over and prepare for the sacrifice of a goat in the sacrificial circle. Using rice flour, the Brahman drew the necessary designs on the ground beside the post. One of the designs was a drawing of a buffalo, since it is the animal most appropriately sacrificed to Durga at this place. The likeness was so poor, even after he had added unmistakable buffalo horns, that it was the butt of many jokes from the small group that stood about. When the kid was to be sacrificed, the father of the Magar boy again acted for him, although the boy himself dragged the body of the goat around the pole and was the one to wet his hands in the goat's blood and plant them so as to leave two handprints on each side of the kot temple door. And finally, he was the one to bring the head of the goat into the temple, and guided by the Brahman set it in the proper place as an offering to Durga. At this time of year in the kot temple the element of force in secular affairs was represented only by one ancient and very rusty sword which was propped against the wall. During the fall ritual many more swords were brought here, including one taken in the last war from a Japanese officer. At that time there also was a bow with some arrows.

THUM LARGESSE

Following the sacrifice, the Hill Village headman went to the pole, placed a rupee on it, and stepped back. Then the Metalworker thum messenger stepped up to the pole, bowed to it with his hands before his face, touched it with his forehead, straightened up, and took the rupee. He was followed in turn by the Tailor messenger and the Leatherworker messenger, each of whom also received a rupee placed there by the headman. In this instance, the pole not only stood for the authority vested in the thum as a whole and expressed primarily through the office of headman but also for its largess to those who serve it.

The theme of thum largess is carried out further in the division and distribution of the body of the goat, which was sacrificed in the circle. The division was made by a very old Leatherworker, to the accompaniment of much joking and laughter. He was a master of miming dimwittedness, augmented by senility. There was, however, no doubt, judging from an occasional out-of-character rejoinder and from the amount of the goat he succeeded in retaining for himself despite the continual admonishment of the Hill Village headman, that he was pretending. He held the office of Nek, and besides dividing and distributing kot sacrifices, it was his responsibility to keep the sacrificial circle free of grass.

In the distribution of the goat, a Tailor received the liver, heart, lungs and the rear section of the backbone. He represented the Tailor group that comes with drums, curved copper horns, and twin-reed woodwinds during the fall Dasain festival, accompanying the offering of consecrated flowers and leaves to Durga. A Metalworker was given the forward section of the backbone and the throat. Like the Tailor, he did not have a role to play in this Dasain ritual, but did have in the fall, when he and another Metalworker brought their sharpening wheel to the kot and used it to prepare a sword (it happened to be the Japanese sword) for the sacrifices that were made at that time.

Three legs of the goat were supposed to be divided equally among the eight headmen of the thum. Despite the commands of the Hill Village headman, the Leatherworker made eight miniscule heaps of meat and kept all four legs for himself. Only after a number of reproofs could the headman get him to give up one of the legs, which was for the Newar shopkeeper who in the fall ceremony provided gifts of cloth for the Brahman who officiated at the temple, for the unmarried boy who sacrificed, and for the Hill Village headman who supervised the ritual as a whole.

All the ribs were supposed to be divided into eighty small pieces, each representing the original eighty houses of the thum and standing now for all the present thum houses. The Nek set to work on one rib and whenever he was told he would have to use more because he did not have eighty pieces, he would chop what he had into finer and finer bits. Finally he took all the bits, which amounted to a handful of much-splintered bone, and stuffed them under the eaves of the kot temple. The head of the goat went to the three messengers, who divided it among themselves. They wrapped the portions for the eight headmen in leaves and set out to deliver them.

At the time of the fall ceremony, it is said that a Brahman from either Pandera Thum or, in rotation, one of three neighboring thums, always takes the leg of a sacrificed goat to the present Rajah of Bhirkot. This gesture of allegiance, which I was unable to confirm fully, apparently harks back to a time before the mid-eighteenth century size of the house of Gorkha. At that time, Pandera Thum and the other three thums were part of the chiefdom of Bhirkot, which in turn was part of a very loose alliance called the Chaubisi (24) Lordships.

The ritual that takes place around the kot temple points to important components in the political sphere. In addition to the headman, there are the messengers and those who have roles to play during the fall ceremonies. It is significant, since we are suggesting that this ritual symbolizes thum unity, that all major castes are represented and in addition all houses in the thum. Thum servants perform their duties and receive their remuneration in a small drama that is directed by a headman, who embodies the focal office of the thum. The symbolic presence of force, represented by weapons, also serves to heighten the secular and political significance of the ritual. But here at the kot temple, just as at the Barahi shrine, another theme is present, although now the relative strength of the two is reversed. The Brahman and the sacred dominate at the Barahi shrine, while the secular and political dominate at the kot temple. But in neither case is the connection between sacred and secular, Brahman and headman, lost sight of. In the second part of the ritual, the Brahman comes more under the headman's direction and resembles to some extent a retainer. But in both parts of the ritual, as in the day-to-day life of the thum, the two spheres—the political and the religious—are mutually supportive and dependent upon each other.

RECENT CHANGES

Banyan Hill and its thum are part of that great shift from an older traditional order that is shaking the modern Asian world—a shift that ultimately, in origin and implications, is not Asian but world-wide.

The Rana family, which ruled Nepal from 1846 to 1951, discouraged education within the country and permitted few to travel or study abroad. Except for a few foreign diplomatic residents of Kathmandu, residence or travel by outsiders was almost nonexistent. These restrictive policies effectively maintained a conservative Hindu policy through the early part of this century. The reformist Hindu sects brought constant pressure on the Rana family for more liberal policies. Prior to their overthrow in 1951 and in the wake of India's successful struggle for independence, the Ranas did make a few moves in liberalized directions. But it was not until the resumption of rule by the Sah family, after the revolution, that the country saw any marked steps in new and more progressive paths.

At this time, especially in the Kathmandu Valley, there was widespread discussion of judicial, political, and economic reform followed by the issuance of a number of government directives. In 1959, with the country's first general election, parliamentary rule was established. The king felt it necessary a year later to dissolve Parliament and rule directly. But by this time, most of the trends in liberal government were established and continued to be encouraged and strengthened.

The most rudimentary economic development of Nepal would hardly have been possible without financial and technical assistance from outside the country. Much of the expense is being met by Russia, China, Israel, and India. The United States foreign aid program, which was extended to Nepal in 1951, has since been steadily expanded.

INCREASED MONETIZATION

In recent years, there has been an increased monetization in Banyan Hill and an increase in trade items available in nearby regions. The primary sources of cash are soldiers' salaries, pensions, and interest from money lending. In two generations, the number of soldiers and pensioners in the thum has more than tripled, and much of the interest on the loans of a large-scale moneylender like the Banyan Hill headman are paid by persons from outside the thum.

Another factor of importance in the emerging cash economy is rising prices. Ten years ago a commonly used village measure (*pathi*) of millet, paddy, or maize cost half a rupee, or fifty pice. In the spring of 1961, paddy and maize were selling for 150 pice, millet for 100 pice a *pathi*. And this was a year of good harvests. There has also been a steady rise in population. Figures from land records (although they are to be relied on with caution) suggest that during the past century, the thum's population has increased about fivefold.

In the area generally, these stimuli to trade are seen in the rapid growth of bazaar towns. Of the six stores in Setipul, all but one were started in the last decade. During this time, two tailors moved to the town; a post office, police station, and government-sponsored health center were established.

Most of Pandera Thum's trading is done in Deorali. The first shop was built here twenty-five years ago, with three others being added in the last twelve years. Some idea of the trading possibilities in Deorali at present are shown by the fact that the owner of the largest shop (with an inventory of Rs 25,000) now talks of setting up another some miles north. The largest selling items in these shops are cigarettes and cloth. The most popular cigarette is made in Nepal and carried in from Narayanghat, a town about four days' walk to the southeast; the bulk of the cloth is Indian made. The cloth as well as most other goods are carried in from Butwal.

CONCENTRATION OF WEALTH

With increasing pressures on the land due to the growth in population, the emergent money economy, and intensification of trade, have come new patterns for the concentration of wealth. In the past, the largest concentrations were acquired by Brahmans who worked as petty officials either in district headquarters or in Kathmandu. According to public opinion, the wealthiest man in the thum is a retired Brahman official. Second place goes either to a Brahman official's widow or to the Magar headman of Banyan Hill, whose inherited estate was not very large. To some extent, his wealth is a result of his favored position in respect to labor and to education, including the ability to write legal documents. But mostly it is due to extensive money lending. Unlike the wealthiest thum Brahmans, whose estates mainly reflect the emoluments of office, this estate reflects a local need for cash brought about by increased trade. Some of the larger loans have been made to shopkeepers.

However, the major significance of his new wealth is its link with the growing pressure on land. The disappearance of vacant, cultivable land, combined with increased population, has pushed more and more farms below the level of marginal productivity. In Banyan Hill, land partition among sons has made an increasing number of farms too small to meet subsistence needs. The most common reason for borrowing is simply to meet the need for food. Given such a situation, great advantage lies with the person, such as the Headman, who has means and ability to lend money. Land and money both flow in his direction. This trend is apparent throughout the thum, among the wealthiest Brahmans as well as among Magars who have retired with large pensions.

IMPROVEMENTS IN MAGAR STATUS

In Pandera Thum, the most conspicuous change in the past few decades has been the improvement in Magar status. Since status is a relative concept and it is the local Brahmans who have the highest status, this change emerges most clearly in the context of Magar-Brahman relations. As a group, the Brahmans always have been better educated than Magars. Together with the two other groups who claim relationship with the twice-born castes of India, the Thakuri and the Chetri, the Brahmans have long been part of the ruling Nepalese elite. There always have been many Brahman officials in local district offices. Twenty years ago, at a time when no Magar held a post above the thum level, five Brahmans from the thum held such office. As a result of their religious, educational, and political advantages, Brahmans, in contrast to Magars, have been able to secure more and choicer land. Less favored groups of the community, including many Magars, are dependent on the Brahmans for labor opportunities and for loans of cash or grain. Fifty percent of the cash loans in Banyan Hill were made by neighboring Brahmans; in two cases, interest on the loan is being paid off by working as a farmhand. It is against such a background that the change in Magar status is to be understood.

A reliable Banyan Hill Magar informant, now in his sixties, estimated that when he was a boy there were only four or five educated Magars in Pandera Thum. In Banyan Hill today there are twenty-eight males and seven females who have had some education. In accounting for this advance, the Banyan Hill headman and Magar soldiering have made important contributions.

Seventeen years ago, the Banyan Hill headman, who had educated himself with the help of Brahman friends, founded a *pathshala* in the thum bazaar. Two of his sons had been attending the thum's first *pathshala,* but it was far away; he felt that his section of the thum should have a school. He provided the building and paid for the services of, first, one *pandit* and then two. Eventually about twenty-five students were attending, half of them Magar and half Brahman. This school ran successfully until the *pandits* said they did not believe Magars should learn the ancient Hindu scriptures, or Vedas. This annoyed the Headman. He closed the school, hired another *pandit,* and began educating his own sons and a few other Magars in his own home. For some years after this, until 1952, Magar education did not receive much imeptus locally. In 1952, with funds he himself provided and with the help of labor he was able to secure, the Headman erected a new, larger building and hired two teachers, including a *pandit,* to staff it. This development was an important factor in making it possible to found a school shortly afterwards with financial assistance from an army-connected source outside the thum.

Army service has made a contribution of long standing. In Banyan Hill, of the sixteen men who are now forty years old or older, ten served in the British army; during the course of their service nine learned to read and write. An army-connected source of education, important for the boys of the present generation, are the schools of Dehra Dun, India, where there is a large Gurkha cantonment. There is a hostel there for boys with a relative in the service, thus making it possible for a few to go and live cheaply among their own countrymen. Ten Magar young men from the thum, among them the Headman's sons, have attended or are attending this Gurkha Military High School.

Another factor of much importance for Magar education, and one that also has an intimate connection with Magar soldiering, is the Central Co-ordination Board Post-War Reconstruction Fund. The fund was established by the government of India for the resettlement of Indian military personnel who had served in World War II. Nepal received its share of the fund in 1952; the money is allocated by a Central Co-ordinating Board acting in cooperation with Zonal Advisory Boards and District Soldiers' Boards—a structure that draws heavily on ex-servicemen who are elected as representatives from areas of heavy pensioner concentration. Pandera Thum falls within the jurisdiction of the Pokhara Zonal Advisory Board and District Soldiers' Board.

One of the uses for the money from the Post-War Reconstruction Fund is the establishment of schools, over which the District Soldiers' Board exercise administrative and financial control. In Pokhara, there is a large, well-staffed District Soldiers' Board High School; four years ago the District Soldiers' Board, acting on a petition from Pandera Thum pensioners, agreed to pay the salaries of two teachers. At present this school has a teaching staff of three middle-aged Magar pensioners from the thum; they have been joined by the young India-educated son of the Banyan Hill headman, who hopes to become headmaster pending Board approval of the petition for his hiring.

The effects of these new and local educational opportunities are clear. Only one literate Banyan Hill man over forty received an education from some source other than soldiering. In contrast, one finds that none of the eighteen literate Banyan Hill males under forty learned to read and write in the army.

With the establishment of the new government in 1951, education for girls was officially encouraged. The effects of this encouragement and the existence of the local school show up in the data on Banyan Hill women. Whereas none of the nineteen village women forty or over are literate, there are seven young girls who have had some education or now are studying.

In Pandera Thum fifty years ago, there was no one Magar family that could compete in prominence with a number of Brahman families. Today this is not true, for now the Banyan Hill headman and his family have attained a prominence that equals or exceeds that of any local Brahmans. In the rough and tumble village politics, this Headman was able to cow all rivals, including the most powerful Brahman clique and three other Magar headmen as well. This brought him well to the fore politically.

In a status system that stresses heredity, ritual equality with Brahmans is not possible for a Magar. But it can be approached, and the Headman has done this. In pursuit of merit, he has undertaken a long series of religiously enjoined activities, most of which have been celebrated in a verse panegyric composed by a Brahman admirer. These include pilgrimages to holy spots; giving his weight in a mixture of gold, silver, and copper to Brahmans; and undertaking mild but very lengthy fasts during which long portions of each day are spent in reciting religious verses. As a result of these activities, his reputation for religiosity equals that of any of the local Brahmans; in fact, there are many local Brahmans with whom he will not eat, since they fail to come up to his standards of ritual purity.

ELEVATING OUTSIDE CONNECTIONS

The example of the Headman is a single case of realignment in Brahman-Magar relations. There also is evidence of a more pervasive change, although it still is in its initial stages. The trend may be summarized in part by stating that many Magars have attained some sort of elevating outside connection or at least are securing the means to such connection. And in this context, there are three areas of special importance to them: the government, the District Soldiers' Board, and the Indian and British armies. The importance of the kind of education now being given in the local schools, and in schools such as the Gurkha Military High School of Dehra Dun, is in its value in securing government employment. As compared with Brahmans, Magars in Pandera Thum are taking greater advantage of this avenue to elevating outside connection.

The District Soldiers' Board, because it is a source of both money and valued service for ex-soldiers (which with few exceptions in Pandera Thum means the Magars), provides another form of elevating outside connection. The District Soldiers' Board Hospital in Pokhara gives priority to ex-soldiers; the Pokhara Soldiers' Board High School, in which one of the India-educated young Magars from Pandera Thum is a teacher, has been established especially for their children.

Finally, the Magars are improving their position through enlistment in the British and Indian armies. There is some ambiguity here, since they serve as mercenaries and often are forced to leave their farms because of poverty. But the ambiguity is slight, and it disappears if the soldier returns as a Gurkha commissioned officer (British) or a junior commissioned officer (Indian). There is even less ambiguity when a man, as is possible now, returns as a retired commissioned officer like the thum's Captain. Few decisions of local importance are made without consulting him, and his village is known as "the Captain's village."

The local connection of most importance for the general enhancement of Magar standing is with the Banyan Hill headman. It is not as a symbol of highest

Magar attainment that he is primarily valued. His Brahmanization, perhaps, is too excessive. The names of Magars from outside the thum—a politician elected as a Nepali Congress representative to Parliament from a nearby district, and a retired Captain from some distance away who has done much to improve his village—are names most mentioned when Magars are asked what member of their group they admire most. But there is widespread agreement that the Headman, besides what he has done to help the education of Magars, has made a helpful contribution of a different kind to their welfare and enhanced stature. He has provided them with protection against families that were taking advantage of them in financial matters. Wealthy Magars were not blameless, but the main source of trouble was a few Brahmans. In the village parlance, these people now are "quiet."

The outcome of the recent general election also was a contribution to general Magar advance. To a large extent, the election turned on a contest between a candidate supported by the Magars and one supported by the Brahmans. The Magar candidate won handily; although Parliament was dissolved before much could be done in the area, Magars did feel, during the time it was in existence, that they were represented by a man interested in their welfare. Winning the election gave Magars an increased sense of their solidarity and, at the same time, gave them a sense of their power, at least under an electoral system.

The Future

Thinking of the future, two trends would seem to have special significance. At present there are virtually no landless families and there is little hunger. Some families eat maize often and rice seldom, but it is possible, by utilizing the land they own, by working for hire, and by borrowing grain or money when times are difficult, for almost all families to get enough to eat. There are wide disparities in wealth, but there is a point beyond which few families have been pushed. One might call it the line of minimal economic sufficiency and self-respect.

The lack of destitute landless helps to create a context in which the "grass roots democracy" the government hopes for will have a better chance of realization. But it seems unlikely that this condition can be maintained in the face of the present trend toward concentration of wealth, a trend which will become more pronounced if this area (through the improvement of transportation facilities) should become a "bread-basket" for the rapidly growing town of Pokhara. Growing pressures on the land and more commercialization of agriculture will erode the existing social controls that prevent poor yeoman farmers from becoming landless laborers. These social controls will be further weakened if the present large landholders, as they become more wealthy, also become absentee landlords. (Already the Headman owns a commerical farming venture in the distant lowlands, and it seems highly probable that in the future one of his sons will want to work it with tenant labor and live in the town or city with his wife and children.) The government is not unaware of these problems and has taken steps toward land reforms and cheap rural credit. But more vigorous action is needed to stem the present trend effectively; such action will become especially imperative if, for any reason, employment opportunities outside the country were to disappear.

The second trend is the growing leadership potential that can be counted on to respond to government guidance. This leadership seems likely to come in greatest strength from the Magars. This is because the general Magar advance not only seems to have been the most far-reaching change in the last decades, but also seems to point in directions encouraged by the government.

The quality of the general Magar advance may be seen most clearly when contrasted with the rise of the Magar Headman. Paradoxically, even though the Headman has made contributions of a high order to the general Magar advance, in its total configuration his rise looks in a different direction. Its main tenor is traditional India and Nepal.

The Magar advance, seen apart from the Headman, has a somewhat different import. Its prime support is foreign military service, and its major activity is education. It is typified by ex-soldiers, who support the new school or participate directly as teachers, and by young men who have been educated above the primary level. Both groups, but more especially the young men, are an important channel through which new ideas, particularly those generated during the course of India's increasingly rapid development, reach the hills. It seems reasonable to expect that this group, which looks more toward a developing than a traditional India and Nepal, will be an increasingly useful source of support for government programs.

Glossary

Aunsi: The new moon

Banyan: A large spreading deciduous tree that sends down many aerials from its branches to the ground. Like the pipal, it is a sacred tree of Hinduism; in contrast to the pipal it is thought to represent the male principle. When planted near the pipal, as is often done, a marriage ceremony sometimes is performed, joining the two trees as if they were man and wife

Bai: The earthbound spirit of an ancestor

Bali: The major biannual postharvest payment families give their service-caste retainers

Barahi: A personification of the energy of Shiva, conceived of as a female consort

Black Bhairam: A manifestation of Shiva

Chaiti-sauni: Two postharvest payments some farmers give their service-caste retainers around March–April (*chaiti*) and July–August (*sauni*)

Cheli-beti: Married daughters and sisters

Damai: A member of the Tailor Untouchable group in the Napalese caste system

Dasain: The major festival period of the Nepalese year. Occurring after the rainy season at the time of the fall harvest, it consists of nine days and nights sacred to Durga, a goddess associated with arms and warfare

Dhansar: A raised open-sided platform with a thatched roof

Durga: A personification of the energy Shiva, conceived of as a female consort. She is associated with arms and warfare

Gharti: A member of the Touchable manumitted or emancipated slave group in the Nepalese caste system. Slaves not already freed by their masters were freed in 1924 by government decree

Guru: A teacher, religious advisor, or song leader

Gurung: A member of a group with Mongoloid physical characteristics and having a Tibeto-Burman house language. They live in the mountains of central Nepal and show strong Buddhist influences. With the Magars, they form the backbone of British and Indian Gurkha regiments

Hukdar: A man's *hukdar* are all men who are descended through male links from the apical ancestor who is six generations removed from himself

Jari: A once married woman who has left her husband and remarried

Jaisi Brahman: A member of the Nepalese priestly caste but of lower status than the Upadhyaya Brahman and not qualified to conduct Vedic rites such as *sraddha.* Many work as astrologers

Jajman: The family or group of families forming the clientele of a Brahman priest

Jhankri: A small deciduous tree with long slender leaves

Kahaura: A Magar song and dance

Kami: A member of the Metalworker Untouchable group in the Nepalese caste system

Kot: The site of the thum fortress and shrines

Krishna: The eighth and most important incarnation of Vishnu

Kutumba: A term usually referring to the husbands of lineage daughters and sisters

Lakshmi: The consort of Vishnu; goddess of wealth and good fortune

Madat: Work done for one's relatives with no expectation of return other than meals

Maita: A wife's natal lineage and village

Mari: The earthbound spirit of a person, other than a soldier, who met a violent end

Mama: Mother's brother

Mamali: Lineage and homeplace of the mother's brother

Nek: A Leatherworker in Pandera Thum with the responsibility of dividing and distributing kot sacrifices and of keeping the sacrificial circle free of grass

Nemiki: Work done for wages

Newar: A member of the Tibeto-Burman–speaking group that from ancient times formed the bulk of the population of the Valley of Nepal, the site of the present capital city of Kathmandu. Newar artisans were responsible for the remarkable artistic achievements of Nepalese civilization

Orni: Tiffin or a snack. Usually parched maize and beer

Pandit: A very learned Brahman

Pathi: One *pathi* of paddy weighs approximately six pounds and of millet and maize, approximately eight pounds

Pathshala: A school emphasizing Sanskrit and religion

Pewa: A gift given by parents to a daughter over which she has sole right

Pice: A small copper coin. One hundred pice equal a rupee. In rituals, it is used to symbolize the presence of Shiva

Pipal: A large deciduous tree with a pale trunk. It is one of the sacred trees of Hinduism and is believed to represent the female principle. It has a heart-shaped leaf

Pitri: Ancestors

Pitri-aunsi: A fortnight following a full moon when ancestors are worshipped

Porima: Work done in exchange for similar kinds of work

Puja: An act of worship. It may vary in elaborateness and length

Pujari: An officiant at an offering, generally a young, unmarried boy

Purne: The full moon

Purohit: A learned Brahman, but less learned than a *pandit*

Rajput: A member of the Indian Warrior or Kshatriya order, the traditional rulers and fighters, ranking next to the order of Brahman priests. In Nepal, the Thakuri caste, of which the present king is a member, has Kshatriya status and claims descent from Indian Rajputs

Ramayana: One of the two great Indian epics

Rana: A member of a division of the Chetri caste, which is part of the Nepalese Kshatriya order. This group produced the hereditary prime ministers who were the de facto rulers of Nepal from 1846 to 1951. In Nepalese pronunciation and orthography there is a slight difference between the word for a Chetri Rana and a Magar Rana. Among the Magars, Rana is the name of a subtribe, like Thapa

Rodighar: Special huts where young people used to gather and sing

Rupee: A coin. One U.S. dollar equals 7.6 Nepalese rupees

Rs: Abbreviation for rupees (q. v.)

Saghau: Work done on special holy days with no expectation of return

Sal: A common broadleaf whose timber provides much building material. The leaves are often used for making leaf plates

Saraswati: A goddess, wife of Brahma, a high Hindu god. She is patron of music, arts and letters

Sari: A woman who has left two husbands and married a third

Sarki: A member of the Leatherworker Untouchable group in the Nepalese caste system

Satya Narayan: A ceremony conducted by a Brahman for the worship of Vishnu

Shiva: Most people in Banyan Hill are worshippers of Shiva, or Shaivites

Sinjali: A Thapa Magar clan

Sraddha: An ancient Hindu ceremony in which ancestral spirits are offered balls of cooked rice to comfort them in the afterworld

Susural: The term used for a wife's natal lineage and village if these are not the same as her mother's

Thapa: A Magar subtribe

Thum: An administrative subdivision

Tikka: An emblem of some kind worn on the forehead, usually placed there during a ceremony as an indication that one has participated, and as an expression of hope for good fortune

Tivahar: A festival period following Dasain and included in the same general period of visiting, feasting, and religious observance. During Tivahar, there is much open gambling; Lakshmi, consort of Vishnu and goddess of wealth and good fortune, is worshipped

Upadhyaya Brahman: A member of a division of the Nepalese priestly caste

Upret: A Brahman regularly providing religious services to a family

Vishnu: A high Hindu god. Some people in Banyan Hill are followers of Vishnu, or Vaishnavites

Yajur Veda: One of the ancient holy texts of Hinduism. It contains sacrificial formulae in prose and verse

Recommended Reading

Nepal

BARNOUW, VICTOR, 1955, Eastern Nepalese Marriage Customs and Kinship Organization. *Southwestern Journal of Anthropology*, 11:15–30.

> Marriage customs of the Rais, based on information obtained in Darjeeling, India. Together with Magars, Gurungs, and Limbus, Rais formed most of the Gurkha Brigade.

FÜRER-HAIMENDORF, C. von, 1964, *The Sherpas of Nepal: Buddhist Highlanders*. London: John Murray.

> An excellent account of the hillmen who figure in mountaineering ventures, by the doyen of anthropologists who write on Nepal.

———, 1960, Caste in the Multi-Ethnic Society of Nepal. *Contributions to Indian Sociology*, 4:12–32.

> The variations of the caste system peculiar to Nepal.

———, 1956, Elements of Newar Social Structure. *The Journal of the Royal Anthropological Institute of Great Britain and Ireland*, 86:15–38.

> Contains much material on the society of the Tibeto-Burman-speaking creators of Nepalese civilization.

GORER, GEOFFREY, 1938, *Himalayan Village: An Account of the Lepchas of Sikkim*, London: Michael Joseph.

> Gorer based his account on fieldwork in Sikkim, but what he says should apply to Lepchas across the border in Nepal.

HAN, SUYIN, 1958, *The Mountain is Young*. London: Jonathan Cape.

> A novel whose early chapters give the gossipy version current in the western community of some of the recent Kathmandu political scene.

HITCHCOCK, JOHN T., 1961. A Nepalese Hill Village and Indian Employment. *Asian Survey*, 1(9):15–20.

> More details on the meaning of Indian employment, and especially army service, to the Magars of Banyan Hill.

————, 1963, Some Effects of Recent Change in Rural Nepal. *Human Organization,* 22(1):75–82.

> More details on changes in Pandera Thum.

————, 1965, Sub tribes in the Magar Community in Nepal. *Asian Survey,* 5(4):207–215.

> Problems of interpretation presented by the Magar sub-tribes.

———— and Patricia Hitchcock, Four films produced under a grant from the Course Content Improvement Program, National Science Foundation. 16mm., color and sound. The first three form a trilogy showing aspects of the culture of Gharti and Pun Magars living in the northern section of the Magar homeland. The fourth was made in Pandera Thum.

> *Fieldwork in Social Anthropology* (45 min.). Begins with the search for a transhumant Magar community; and once it is found, shows some of the problems and pleasures of carrying out research there. The film answers many questions the author is asked frequently about fieldwork in Nepal.
>
> *Himalayan Farmer* (22 min.), An example of ecological adaptation which also is a "cultural trap." In carrying out a difficult basic daily routine, a farmer reveals much about himself, his family, and his community.
>
> *Himalayan Shaman of Northern Nepal* (16 min.). The curing methods of the Siberian type of shaman found among northern Magars. This is probably one of the most southerly points of penetration of this complex. The shaman, shown curing Magars, is a Metalworker.
>
> *Himalayan Shaman of Southern Nepal* (14 min.) A working day in the life of the foremost Magar shaman of Pandera Thum. One sees his diagnosis and treatment of patients by spirit possession and by use of medicines that show the influence of traditional Hindu practice.

KARAN, P. PRADYUMNA, *Nepal: A Cultural and Physical Geography.* 1960. Lexington: University of Kentucky Press.

> In addition to much geographical information, provides a good overview of many aspects of Nepalese culture and history. Many maps.

KIHARA, HITOSI (ed.), 1955, *Peoples of Nepal Himalaya.* III. Kyoto University, Kyoto: Fauna and Flora Research Society.

> Ethnographic notes of varying validity by a Japanese scientific expedition that traveled through parts of Nepal inhabited by Magars. The relation made between culture and environmental features is useful and suggestive.

MASTERS, JOHN, 1956, *Bugles and a Tiger: A Volume of Autobiography.* New York: Viking.

> The book gives a lively picture of Gurkha troops in British India and tells how a gifted officer learned his profession prior to the Second World War.

————, 1961, *The Road Past Mandalay: A Personal Narrative.* London: Michael Joseph.

A moving continuation of *Bugles and a Tiger,* with an account of Gurkha troops in action during the Burma Campaign.

NORTHEY, W. BROOK AND C. J. MORRIS, 1928, *The Gurkhas: Their Manners, Customs and Country.* London: John Lane.

Contains material for use of British officers serving with Gurkha troops. There is a chapter on Magars and their neighbors, the Gurungs. Chapter IV, by R. L. Turner, discusses the languages of Nepal.

OKADA, FERDINAND E., 1957, Ritual Brotherhood: A Cohesive Factor in Nepalese Society. *Southwestern Journal of Anthropology,* 13:212–222.

An account of ritual brotherhood among various groups in Nepal and suggestions about its function.

SNELLGROVE, D. L., 1957, *Buddhist Himalaya.* Oxford: Bruno Cassirer.

Contains an excellent chapter on Buddhism in Nepal.

TUKER, SIR FRANCIS, 1957, *Gorkha: The Story of the Gurkhas of Nepal.* London: Constable.

A history of Nepal, written with nostalgia for the period of Empire but with emphasis on mountain tribes and castes recruited for the Gurkha Brigade.

General

BERREMAN, GERALD D., 1963, *Hindus of the Himalayas.* Berkeley and Los Angeles: University of California Press.

A study that brings out similarities and differences between a hill community in the Dehra Dun District of North India and the society and culture of the Indian plains.

BURLING, ROBBINS, 1963, *Rengsanggri.* Philadelphia: University of Pennsylvania Press.

Describes the Garos, who are Tibeto-Burman–speaking and one of the largest hill tribes of Assam. Discusses cross-cousin marriage in a matrilineal society.

CARRASCO, PEDRO, 1959, *Land and Polity in Tibet.* Seattle: University of Washington Press.

Brings together and organizes a wide range of sources on Tibet that are not easily accessible.

REDFIELD, ROBERT, 1956, *Peasant Society and Culture.* Chicago: University of Chicago Press.

A classic analysis of the type of society and culture the Magars represent.